A
LONDON FAMILY
BETWEEN
THE WARS

A
LONDON FAMILY
BETWEEN
THE WARS

*

M. V. Hughes

Oxford   New York   Toronto   Melbourne
OXFORD UNIVERSITY PRESS
1979

Oxford University Press, Walton Street, Oxford OX2 6DP

OXFORD LONDON GLASGOW
NEW YORK TORONTO MELBOURNE WELLINGTON
KUALA LUMPUR SINGAPORE JAKARTA HONG KONG TOKYO
DELHI BOMBAY CALCUTTA MADRAS KARACHI
NAIROBI DAR ES SALAAM CAPE TOWN

First published by Oxford University Press 1940.
First issued as an Oxford University Press paperback 1979

British Library Cataloguing in Publication Data

Hughes, Mary Vivian
    A London family between the wars.
    1. London – Social life and customs
    I. Title
    942.1'083'0924 DA688   79–40775

ISBN 0–19–281277–7

Reproduced, printed and bound in Great Britain by
Cox & Wyman Ltd, Reading

PREFACE

THE words 'London' and 'Family' are as common and prosaic as any in the language. But each has a mystic quality. London is not so much a place as an idea. Some years ago an Englishman in America had to state his birthplace, and put down 'London'. 'Eng. or Ont. ?' he was asked. 'Neither,' said he, 'London the whole blooming world.' When Mr. Churchill said in his broadcast to the nation, 'We would rather see London laid in ruins and ashes than that it should be tamely enslaved', he knew that he could say nothing better calculated to steel our hearts for endurance and make us laugh with delight. Yes, delight in sacrifice and death, for something better, some deep unspoken glory.

And the word 'Family' implies much more than a collection of people tied by relationship. Differences of character and opinion, the stress of poverty, bits of success, days of fun, accidents and illness, long and heart-rending separations, even death itself—all serve to bind its members closer, and charge the word with lovelier meaning as life grows sterner.

There are millions of London families, many of them scattered now over the world. This is the story of twenty years in the life of a commonplace one.

CONTENTS

A Greek Gift

'Don't worry, dear. Boys always come home to supper.'

These words, absurdly cheering, came from an old lady, a neighbour during my happy married days in Barnet, and the cause of my worry was this: the first German Zeppelin had been brought down at a place called Cuffley, and the world at large was flocking to 'have a look' at the spot. Among them were my three boys, aged sixteen, twelve, and eight. The eldest knew all there was to know about trains, and the younger ones were game for any adventure. It was still holiday time and fine September weather, so I had packed them off early with sandwiches, and the injunction 'Take care of Arthur' (the youngest).

When evening came on I had to fix my mind on Hans Andersen's story of the mother eel, and it was a great relief to see them straggling in, tired and hungry, but quite full of the day's doings. The only information they had about Cuffley was this: jolly, quite in the country, and the station was a sort of terminus—at least the trains stopped there because the line on to Hertford had been left unfinished when the war began.

The whole incident passed out of my mind.

After eighteen months more of happiness I was suddenly left a widow. Fortunately there was very little money. It was fortunate because I was crazy with grief, and the necessity to work kept me going. Having found a teaching job, I gave up our house in Barnet, sold much of the furniture, and moved into a suburban flat nearer my work. One day a young friend came to see me. She and her husband had been among the sightseers at Cuffley, and had been so charmed with the place that they had hunted about for some kind of dwelling.

'You can hardly call it a house,' said she, 'and yet it isn't a cottage. About a hundred yards from the station, up a tiny lane, we found eight semi-detached little gabled villas. They had been built for the men superintending the railway works. Of course they were no longer wanted when the work stopped. But the shortage of houses soon filled them again.'

'What sort of people?' I asked.

'Oh,' she laughed, 'an odd collection.'

'Then how did you manage to get one?'

'The people in one of them had had to leave.'

'Fleeing from justice?' I suggested.

'Quite possibly—but anyhow it was luck for us. Do come to see it.'

When I reached the spot one summer afternoon I found that Mrs. Hart's description had been an understatement. The little houses, although so close to the station, were in completely unspoiled country—trees and fields whichever way I looked. I was determined to lay all plans for coming here. The first point to settle was the train journey for the boys to get to Merchant Taylors' School. That was not bad; the first train left a little after 8 a.m., and they could get back about 5 p.m., and they always had dinner at school.

As for my own work it could be managed as easily from Cuffley as from London, for I had given up teaching in school for work of a different kind—inspecting and examining.

The only trouble was to find an empty house.

Inquiries led to a possibility. One pair of houses was owned by a man who used only the half, because the adjoining house was in disrepair. He was willing to sell me this latter very cheaply if I would take it as it was. It was in the best position of all, with unbroken view of open fields and a great spreading oak in its front garden. The repairs were not very extensive. I thought my funds might manage it. I had saved a little money; my husband's kindhearted solicitor had screwed from various clients the fees long overdue; my eldest son, Vivian, had gained a good scholarship at B.N.C. and I felt capable of working until my youngest son should be on his own feet. So the little house became mine.

'Estimate' is a curious word. In my experience it has always meant 'understatement' when used by builders and furniture removers. They find, when they come to do the job, that they had not realized the extent of the work required or of the amount of goods to be moved. And a woman is fair game for them. As for their estimate of time —I think there should be a super-heated department in the future life, with no water laid on, for those builders who name a false date for the end of their work.

My repairing builder named a date in early September 1920 for the house to be ready. In the morning of the appointed date a big lorry stood at the door of our London home, and our furniture was pushed into it. When it was ready to start, my youngest boy, Arthur, got up beside the driver with our Welsh terrier, Lerry, and the thing lumbered off, leaving Vivian and me to bring the four last things and some food. My middle son, Barnholt, had already started on his bicycle, with a school friend, who was coming to help.

The lorry and the bicycles outran the train, and consequently Vivian and I were met at the station by the other boys. This would have been splendid if their first words had not been:

'Everything is in chaos.'

This was hardly an exaggeration. The workmen were stolidly engaged in their 'building and decorating' job, so that we could not even enter the larger of the two bedrooms. The removers were pushing in the furniture as fast as they could (since it was piecework) and displaying the usual disregard, or humorous regard, of the appropriate places. I caught sight of a hairbrush in the meat-safe and two volumes of the *Encyclopaedia Britannica* among the blankets, to name only two of the oddities. All the boys, of course, were bending with the removers to remove, while I concentrated on the commissariat. There was no room to eat in the house, but it was glorious weather, and I laid out the eggs, sandwiches, and fruit on a log in the back garden. The schoolfellow had thoughtfully acquired some ginger-beer, and as soon as the lorry had gone we all fell to, and were soon laughing heartily at the 'chaos'.

The supply of food was naturally my chief concern, so while the boys were placing the furniture into some sort of order, I set about making inquiries. Unfortunately my

4

friends, the Harts, were on their summer holiday, but our semi-detached neighbour told me that a baker from Northaw (about a mile away) called every day with bread, a farm near by brought milk, and one of the neighbours kept fowls and would be glad to have a customer for her eggs.

'You are quite welcome,' she added, 'to anything we have grown in your part of the garden, but everything else has to be fetched from Enfield.'

In a few days' time we were able to congratulate ourselves, not only on breathing country air, but on enjoying three warm things: milk warm from the cow, bread warm from the oven, and eggs warm from the nest. And I lost no time before exploring the garden. I found two rows of scarlet runners, and a grand mine of potatoes, as well as carrots, parsley, and mint.

With such alleviations to the emergency tin of corned beef that I had brought from London, we managed for a day or two—'dining heavily on scraps', as a friend of mine once described those odd meals at which one usually overeats.

The two elder boys busied themselves putting down stair-carpet, arranging the books into the cases, hanging up the pictures, and (wisely, I think) quietly decreasing the ornaments. 'No sentimentality, mother', was their sensible slogan. In such ways they 'cleared a little space' like Sir Lancelot. But Arthur used to disappear for an hour or so at a time, and return with grand spoil of blackberries or mushrooms, or both—welcome additions to our larder.

'Larder' was hardly the word for the hole under the stairs, and as for the kitchen, it was no more than a passage between the window and the bath, which was covered so as to serve as a kitchen table. However, the big sitting-room was soon a delight, with windows at each end, books, pictures, and some comfortable chairs. We had our meals at whichever end the mood fancied.

My visit to Enfield became a weekly duty, for stocking the larder with meat, butter, cheese, and usually fruit, vegetables, and fish. I took two vast baskets, and often enough could only just stagger from the town to the station with my load. At the Cuffley end it was not so bad, for I could take one load at a time. It was safe to leave anything anywhere in Cuffley; if you were going to town, starting with an umbrella, and then changed your mind about the weather prospect, you could push the umbrella in a hedge and collect it on your return.

There was no shop of any kind, but there were two important substitutes. The postman, on a bicycle, brought me *The Times* every morning. A friendly fellow he was, and on a very cold morning would come in for a cup of coffee. The other boon was a hawker with a pony-cart, calling once a week. He was known as the 'cotton man', because he always had sewing-materials. I hailed him as though he was an albatross, not that sewing-materials attracted me, but because he carried almost everything else —soap, candles, matches, sugar, rice, tinned fruit, socks and stockings, underwear, handkerchiefs, blouses, and even dresses. Also he could procure and bring for me any article that was difficult (or unseemly) for me to carry from Enfield, such as a big washing-bowl, a doormat, or a fire-guard.

6

One day this Mr. Harris was missing at his accustomed hour, but appeared in the late afternoon, full of very low-toned apology, thus:

'I'm sorry, mum, to be a bit behind-like, but the missus is expecting, and I had to stay with her. . . .'

That was nineteen years ago, and Mr. Harris still comes. Often he has brought the expected one with him—now in a job of his own.

The railway and its personnel were at first our chief contacts with the outside world. We soon knew all the possible trains: the earliest started a little after 8 in the morning, and the last left King's Cross at 9 p.m. 'You must be very moral people in Cuffley,' was the remark of my inspecting chief on hearing about these conditions. 'No theatres, no dances, no London nights of any kind, virtuous or otherwise!'

One Saturday evening Barnholt failed to appear by the 9 p.m. He had been away at football and gone home with a schoolfellow probably. It was no use worrying about it, for he was quite capable of looking after himself. But just as I was going to bed he burst in with the glad news that a late train had been put on for Saturdays, leaving King's Cross at 10.

This was an unexpected concession, for the patrons of the line were few. Civilization stopped at Gordon Hill, a suburban district of Enfield. Here the world got out, most trains reversed, as very few went the extra bit to Cuffley. Since we were sure of not being carried too far, we were often glad to fall asleep after a tiring day. But some busybody in the carriage would be only too likely to ask, with a tap on the knee, 'Do you know where you are going?'

We were well known to the booking-clerks and porter, and a train would be held a bit if we were seen running. As our little lane ran straight up to the railway embankment, Barnholt would sometimes cut the station, dash up the lane, and jump into the off-side of the train. The boys had season-tickets, but my journeys to town were rare enough to arouse curiosity—sometimes first-class, sometimes third-class. It always seems to me the friendliest (and also most disarming) thing to meet curiosity with frank explanation; after all, there are few things in life that call for reserve. So one morning, after saying, 'King's Cross, please, first,' I added, 'You see I am expected to go first when I am working for the University.' After that, the clerk would say when I mentioned King's Cross, 'Work or play?' and pass me the appropriate ticket. If it was play, I would add my objective, perhaps some shop or a matinée. After all, why not?

Occasionally I ran it close and got into the train without a ticket. The collector at King's Cross would look at me with curiosity when I announced that I had come from Cuffley, first-class.

'I have *heard* of Cuffley,' was the usual response, but he would make no bones about taking my word for it, and the fare (for which he had to consult his book of words).

My inspection work would sometimes take me away for a few days at a time, for it ranged over places as far away as Northumberland, Lancashire, Devon, Norfolk, and the Channel Islands. But the bulk of my work could be done at home, for it consisted in setting papers, correcting scripts, and inspecting examinations set and corrected by teachers. The quiet of Cuffley was just the thing for writing reports on all these things. One old fellow attached to the station had reason to wish my work otherwise, for he had to bring immense parcels of scripts to my door in his pony-cart. He was far too feeble to lift them, and I had to take one end of each parcel, to drag it into the house.

The boys were dispersed—Vivian to Oxford, and the other two to school. It was Arthur's first term at Merchant Taylors'. He confided to me one evening that he had rather dreaded being ragged by the other boys, because when excited or nervous he had a slight stammer.

'But it was all right, Mother. I did stammer a bit over doing a proposition, and had the boys closing round me afterwards. But they were cheering me to further efforts—because I had delayed the lesson.'

So the stammer was an asset, it seemed. But of course its very success killed it.

When I had once seen the boys off to school, and settled what the evening meal was to be, I could arrange my work as I liked, and had plenty of time for walks and finding out the lie of the land. Up the hill across the fields I found the original hamlet of Cuffley, consisting of six old cottages, a small green with a pump, the *Plough* Inn, an old farmhouse with a beautiful tiled barn attached to it, and a painfully ugly corrugated-iron church. Near this was the stone column erected to the memory of Leefe Robinson, who had brought down the Zeppelin, in 1916.

I preferred to wander along our ill-laid road right on

into a lane, and then to strike into the grassy paths of a lovely wood. For the first time I began to feel alive after two years' misery. And my constant companion, Lerry, seemed to become a puppy again, as he leapt along chasing imaginary rabbits. One day I lost my direction among the many paths; so I sat down, and Lerry flung himself panting beside me. After a rest I said firmly, 'Home, Lerry!' Immediately he started off, and I meekly followed. How charming, I felt, to be *able* to lose my way, and to have a dog who could find it!

One night I woke to notice a curious light on the horizon. The moon was setting among a glory of silver clouds. I stared in stupid amazement. I had seen many a fine sunset, but never before (or since) a moonset. In fact, I am coining the word, for the *O.E.D.* doesn't mention it, although quite chatty about a sunset.

So long accustomed had I been to town life in respectable roads that I felt the relief of being able to walk forth at any moment, in any comfortable clothes that wouldn't suffer from brambles, in thick shoes, and usually hatless. Beyond the garments appropriate for inspection work, I gave no thought to clothes. And the boys were well fortified in this direction, because an old friend who had precisely the same boys as myself, only a stage older, passed on their suits in excellent condition. This led to an odd situation once. The Flemmings took a country cottage in a neighbouring county, and wrote that they would be glad to see any of us who cared to walk over; directions were given, and Barnholt replied that he would come on the following Sunday afternoon. Now the boys didn't know one another, so one of the Flemmings was posted to walk along the lane and keep a lookout for someone about his own age who appeared to be not quite sure of his objective. What was his surprise to see one of his own suits walking along!

'Ah, Hughes, how do you do?' he called out.

I need hardly say that the grounds of recognition were not breathed, and it was only from Mrs. Flemming later on that I had the story.

For some time now Barnholt had become one of the head form at school, and as such was privileged to wear a bowler instead of the 'lamb and flag' cap. His bowler, a pass-on to begin with, had come to look weary and indeed disgraceful. I suggested that we should rise to a new one.

'No, no,' he cried, 'not on your life! Why, Hughes's bowler is one of the standard jokes of the school.'

It will be seen that the boys were wholeheartedly with me in the enjoyment of our carefree, unshopsoiled, country life, in this gem of a spot, only some fifteen miles from Charing Cross.

I have called Cuffley a Greek Gift, because of its unique origin. Towns have had a great variety of origins: river-mouths, hill-tops, shrines, wells, oases, cross-roads, mining-districts, and so forth. None but Cuffley owes its development, from a hamlet into an embryo township, entirely to an unpleasant arrival from the sky. Was this a disaster or a boon? As a family, we have had our home in it for twenty years, the years of peace, and have seen every stage in its growth. My sons have been away for long periods, and travelled far and wide, but their first question on their return is invariably, 'Well, mother, what's the news in Cuffley?'

Except for the absence of a few days at a time on work or holiday, I have been here all through its vicissitudes, and these pages describe the difficulties and delights of my sequestered life in it.

But civilization will keep creeping in. For years I was proud of telling my friends that 'Mrs. Hughes, Cuffley' was sufficient address. The time came when it was safer to put the name of the house, since another Hughes had settled here. And the other day I was told very tartly, by a tele-phone-exchange lady: 'Your future address is to be "19 East Ridgeway"—please inform your correspondents.'

Another symptom of civilization is the appearance of Cuffley in *The Times* crossword. This clue caught my delighted eye: 'An anthropological specimen that might be found in Cuffley. (Two words. 7, 4.)' For those who have no cross-helps I may add that the usual hunting-ground is under the dressing-table.

II

Visitors

WE had been too busy settling in during the first week
or so to give a thought to our human surroundings
beyond our semi-detached and the egg-producer. One
afternoon, therefore, I was a little taken aback to hear a
polite knock on our ever-open front door, and to find a
smartly dressed person with a card in her hand.

'Oh, come in,' I said, 'come in.'

She was hardly seated when she began thus, 'We hope
you will like to join the "Cuffley Ladies"—our little social
circle here.'

Scenting working parties—card parties—musical evenings—my brain had to work quickly. They say that some
juice inside one gets busy when one is in a tight corner.
Well, it did me good service at this moment, for I heard
myself saying,

'I'm so sorry, but I can't join your circle. I can't sew, or
do anything useful, or play cards, or be sociable in any
way; and I'm not a lady.'

It was this last remark that brought her to her feet, and
with a look of almost alarm she confined any further remarks to the weather. I have no doubt that she told her
circle that the new-comer was eccentric. And this was all
to the good. Once establish a character for eccentricity,
and one can do anything.

On the return of Mrs. Hart from her holiday I learned a

good deal more about our neighbours. It seemed that between our semi-detached and the egg-producer there was a feud of such long standing that it had become almost a kind of saga. The cat of our semi-detached would add to the home larder with a chicken. The egg-producer had a reprisal in store; she produced goats as well as eggs, and was accustomed to destroy any unwanted kids 'with horrid personal slaughter' (according to gossip). One day our semi-detached came to me in great indignation.

'Look, that dreadful woman is burning the remains of the kids, and the smoke and smell are pouring into my garden—all over the clothes I've just hung out.'

'That's too bad,' said I, 'she might consider your feelings and watch the way of the wind before starting the fire.'

'She *does* think of my feelings! She *does* watch the wind!'

Needless to say, the children from all the houses played with one another, completely regardless of overhead likes and dislikes. Mrs. Hart had two small girls, one of them only a year old; she was asked one day how she managed about her children when she went to Enfield.

'Oh, that's simple,' said she, hoping to add fuel to the gossip. 'I lock them in a cupboard.'

Curiosity had been aroused because none of us had any servant of the ordinary kind. But the fact was that the Harts had a very efficient servant. During the war they had befriended a Russian refugee, and now he was acting as a kind of batman, doing any odd job—gardening, woodcutting, whitewashing—and was a perfectly reliable nurse for a few hours. He had few English words, and we loved to hear him addressing the Newfoundland dog thus: 'Kom,

kom, mine littel hund,' with no effect on the dog. We
never knew his name, and called him 'Pardon', because he
always prefaced any remark with this word. We would be
sitting at our work in the evening, when suddenly 'Pardon'
would be softly breathed, and this man would materialize
in the room with a laconic request for a hammer or cork-
screw or what not. One day I was sitting in the garden
doing some writing work, when Pardon appeared. His
people were away for the day, and he was evidently in need
of something.

'Pardon! You go Enfield? yes? no?'

'Yes. Do you want something?'

'Pardon! A littel meat—two pound.'

I nodded and he left the presence with a deep bow. I
went on with my work, and after some time he stood before
me again.

'Pardon! Vat I vish is here.' He was bowing profoundly,
with both hands clasping his bosom. For one wild flash I
imagined that it was a proposal of marriage, but reason
rocked back, and I said:

'Yes, I see, you want two pounds of breast of mutton.'

Since this old fellow was the only approach to domestic
service within sight, I remarked to Mrs. Hart how funny it
seemed, what a change from old days, and how pleasant,
to simplify work so that no one needed the cap-and-apron
sisterhood.

'You mustn't suppose that everyone is so simple,' she
replied. 'Up along the Ridgeway, at long intervals, there
are one or two villas, belonging to superior people—one a
retired colonel, one a major, one a kind of important "local

lady", and, a good deal farther on, a wealthy wine-merchant. But all these fancy themselves belonging to Northaw rather than to this mushroom (or is it a toadstool?) Cuffley.'

'Let them keep their Northaw,' said I. 'Give me Cuffley.'

'Ah, but you'll find the local lady will call on you. She makes a point of visiting what she calls "the cottagers".'

Sure enough, she did. A few days later I was on my knees at the open door, trying to fix the always tiresome end of a stair-carpet, when a tall figure loomed up, with 'local lady' written all over her. An elegant voice breathed:

'Is Mrs. Hughes at home?'

'I am sorry to say she is not,' I replied.

'Oh . . . dear me . . . are *you* not Mrs. Hughes?'

'Yes, indeed, but I am not at home.'

'How unlucky! I am so tired after my long walk.'

It was her wit pitted against mine, and she had fairly won.

'Come in, come right in,' said I.

'Books!' she exclaimed in rapture, as though she had glimpsed the Taj Mahal, and immediately we were friends over this never-failing bond.

Among our own little group of 'cottagers' we discovered a much more interesting intellectual. This was an old German named Brand. It was a discovery, for he and his wife had kept very much to themselves, owing to the absurd fear of spies that had arisen during the war and still left a trail of ill-feeling. This old fellow had a flair for mechanics, and kept a mysterious shed in his garden, full of strange contraptions. He had clocks of all kinds, and one that needed winding only once a year. The boys enjoyed looking at his things, and I am sure that he and his wife were glad of our friendship. One evening I was begged to come over, as there was something wonderful to show me. Brand and his wife were excited at some sounds coming over the air. They pressed some instrument on my head and ears, and I certainly heard some strains of what was no doubt distant music. 'This is very wonderful,' I kept repeating, but could detect no pleasure in it, and for a long time paid no more attention to the talk of this new invention. It seemed to me that our own piano, on which the boys amused themselves, was good enough. Mr. Hart had a pianola, a marvellous arrangement for getting a piece of classical music without the trouble of practising. He played Tchaikovski's *Humoresque* grandly, but after a large number of performances I felt like Orsino: 'Enough, no more; 'tis not so sweet now as it was before.'

Sometimes old Brand would bring in his zither to play to us; but as he took the best part of an hour to tune it, we had had enough before the real piece began. A greater endurance test even than this was provided by a school-fellow of Barnholt's, who would bicycle over at any time, sit down firmly at the piano, and play Coleridge Taylor exclusively. He played very badly, and however often he repeated a piece he never improved. I hadn't the heart to stop him, for I fancy his family either had no piano or had driven him forth to preserve their sanity.

Visitors we had in plenty from our own private sources; not only other Merchant Taylor boys, but also old Highgate schoolfellows of Vivian's and his new Oxford friends. My own old schoolfellows, pupils, and students came to see what new prank I was up to, and to lend a helping hand.

As a rule they came by train or bicycle. A car was so rare as to be a local excitement. Our road, indeed, did not attract cars, for it was full of holes, and only 'mended' by the farmer throwing down old half-bricks in the worst places. It chanced that two of my former fellow lecturers on the staff at Whitelands had made the grand adventure of buying a car—an open two-seater. When I described our new surroundings they determined to drive out to see me. A day was fixed for them to come to lunch, and when the hour drew near I told Arthur to go out and watch for them while I saw to the meal. Presently he came running in, looking distressed.

'They've come, mother; but they are still in the car—and quarrelling frightfully.'

I couldn't help laughing, attributing their vexation to hunger. If I had known as much about cars as I do now, I should have put it down to the fact that a joint-owned car had been driven along an unfamiliar course, with advice from the non-driver all the way, and was ending up in our appalling lane.

I had good reason to be horrified by that road before long. Barnholt returned from school on the last day of term with a cold and became feverish. By some means (I forget what) I managed to summon the doctor from Potter's Bar. He diagnosed scarlet fever, and as I had no means of isolation he ordered the ambulance to come and take Barnholt to the fever hospital in Hertford. My feelings can be imagined when I saw that poor boy put on a stretcher in a covered car to be rattled over that road. There was no railway then to Hertford, and when I went to visit Barnholt

I had to walk to Cheshunt and then take the bus. I think the conditions in that hospital according to Barnholt's account would surprise a doctor of to-day.

Fortunately Vivian was away on holiday, and Arthur showed no signs of infection; so things might have been much worse. My next shock was of a different kind. It was term-time, and I was at work at home when a frail-looking little old woman stood at the door with the unmistakable envelope of a telegram in her hand. She had walked all the way across the fields from Northaw, our nearest Post Office. I made her sit down and brought her some refreshment before I had the courage to read the message. It ran, 'Your son ill come at once.'

People should be careful how they word a telegram. That journey of mine to Oxford was a nightmare. But Vivian was neither dead nor dying, and after two days I was able to come home to the others.

These two calamities made me realize how much I had gambled in coming so far from civilization—staking everything on the good health of the four of us. I determined to find some means of reaching the Post Office quickly in any future emergency. Both Barnholt and Arthur had bicycles, and went anywhere for me when they were at home; but I must be more mobile when alone all day. So I made up my mind to learn to ride a bicycle myself.

It chanced that I had been helping the daughter of a neighbour with her Latin (she was trying for some examination), and when she came in next I propounded my idea to her.

'A good idea,' said she, 'and if you can get hold of a

bicycle I shall be delighted to teach you how to ride it; it's quite easy.'

'Easy' is a relative term, surely. Theoretically bicycling is simplicity itself—you sit on and pedal. On a good level road, yes, but I am still amazed to recall how I learned to stick on even for a few yards along that rough lane of ours. However, there was no traffic difficulty to worry about, for if any people appeared I called out, 'I'm a learner—look out!' and they scattered at once. It is no use shouting at a cow or a sheep, so if I saw one of these loitering in the way I dismounted. Again, if I saw someone I knew, I dismounted, for it was dangerous to wave my hand. The road to Northaw was far better in point of surface, but had its own drawbacks. For one thing it was not so much on the level; and I dared not ride downhill in case the brake went out of action; and I could not ride uphill. For another thing I dismounted if I saw a car approaching, for my very terror of it made me somehow attracted to it (I can't account for this). One day I was carefully planning to overtake a working man walking slowly by the hedge, when I saw a car approaching. I must dismount, of course, and immediately found myself, safely dismounted indeed, but on to the shoulder of the working man.

'Never you mind, mum,' was his kind reply to my profuse apology, as he watched me safely off once more.

In short, dismounting was my star turn, and I saw that bicycling as a means of rapid transport was no use to me.

'Yes, but it is such a pleasure,' said Mrs. Hart to me when I mentioned my troubles. 'Come with me to Enfield, and see a bit of the country round.'

She chose a roundabout way, and I thought Enfield would never come, but I struggled painfully after her, suffering more by *not* dismounting than by using my own technique. How glad I was when Enfield was reached, and there was a legitimate reason for dismounting while Mrs. Hart went into the Post Office.

'We had better go home now,' said she on emerging.

'Yes, indeed,' I agreed, 'and by a shorter route if there is one,' remembering the dreadful hill up to Goff's Oak that we had climbed on our way, and would have to go down— a still worse ordeal.

'Oh yes,' was the reply, 'there is a much shorter way, if I can hit it. We'll start up Windmill Hill anyhow.'

After we had been going about a mile (though it felt like three), it came on to rain, and presently Mrs. Hart's voice reached me,

'Sorry, I don't seem to see our turning; we may have passed it. I'll ask someone. We had better go on; we are sure to get somewhere.'

I thought that this was quite possible, but going on was not what I fancied—sticking on was as much as I could manage, and only that with difficulty. Presently I heard,

'Which way to Cuffley, please?'

'You had better turn back, mum—the turning is about half a mile the other way. Of course you *can* get there along this way, but it's much longer.'

Feeling, like Macbeth, that it was easier to go on, whatever the horrors ahead, than to go back to endure those already sampled, I shouted, 'Let's go on.' Anyhow, it wouldn't involve turning.

So on we went, pedalling in the rain, and for what seemed ages life was a grim mist of endeavour to stay the course. When I heard Mrs. Hart exclaim, 'Here's Potter's Bar', in sheer relief I fell with my bicycle into the Great North Road.

Now Potter's Bar is as near Cuffley as makes no matter, for the boys had often just 'run into Potter's Bar' on a bicycle for something. So I mounted again; the rain had stopped; the sun was shining, and I took courage when Mrs. Hart assured me that it was an easy road home. Then for the first time I experienced the beauties of the lane arched by great trees, and the undulating Ridgeway that seemed designed by nature for bicyclists.

I may add here the end of my bicycling achievements. If I had one of the boys with me I was all right, for my chain could be put on if it fell off. But they objected strongly to my going out alone; and when I contemplated doing so, I found that one of them had 'borrowed' one of the wheels. Evidently they believed in drastic measures.

III

Work and Play

OUR quarters in the little house were restricted, but it was a capital place for work. We were none of us noisy in our pursuits, so were able to carry on in our one big sitting-room—with a coal-fire one end and a gas-fire at the other. When Vivian was at home he was reading for his next examination at Oxford. Barnholt was hoping to get an open scholarship, too, and needed some extra coaching. My old friend Ursula Wood gave him a temporary home in London for this purpose. I mention this coaching to show how valuable it was, chiefly because his tutor pointed out to Barnholt what he need *not* worry about. Barnholt's own delight was to explore London and its 'free fountains of culture', as he called the British, Guildhall, London, and other museums, several of which are hard enough to discover. I remember one day in the holidays giving him some sandwiches for such an expedition, to avoid the expense of a lunch in a shop.

'Where did you eat your lunch?' I asked idly when he came home.

'Behind Amenhotep IV,' was the reply.

He went up in due course to try for a scholarship, and to his amazed delight beheld as the subject set for the great essay—'London'. I fancy that his next three hours were complete bliss. Perhaps it was that essay that gained him his scholarship.

Of course the two elder boys were far beyond wanting
any help in their work from me. And Arthur, the youngest,
was threatening to be still more independent of us all, for
his taste was for science—chemistry and physics and things
like that. But now and again, when the other two were
away at Oxford, he was glad of a bit of my help. To his
obvious disgust some preliminary examination required
him to know some Latin, and I could get him on well in
that. There were also lessons in English—most unneces-
sary affairs, in his view. And indeed I began to share his
view, when I saw the things he had to do. One evening,
after tea, he surprised me with,

'I say, mother, do you know anything about the life of
Beethoven?'

'Yes, dear. Ages long ago when I was at school I learnt
that he was born at Bonn. Beyond that useful fact I'm a
blank.'

'Oh, well, I've got to write an essay on him to-night.'

'You can say something about his music, anyway.'

'Oh no, that's no good. It's got to be his life. Never
mind, I'll just get it out of the Encyclopaedia.'

I hoped he would be downcast at the enormous extent
of the Encyclopaedia's information. But not so. He began
at once to copy out the stuff as it came.

'Surely,' said I after a while, 'you are not copying it
exactly?'

'Yes, we've got to do three pages, and it doesn't matter
what it is. He won't read it anyhow.'

As for my own work, that was varied enough to keep
me very much alive mentally. I never went to inspect a

school without bringing back some fresh idea. Huge batches of examination scripts meant arduous work, but were not without some light relief. I made a note of some few answers, and here is a sample from a School Certificate script:

Question: Tell two stories of Saul, showing those weaknesses in his character which caused Samuel to be so grievously disappointed in this first king of the Israelites.

Answer: When Saul was on a journey in the East, the mule which was bearing him suddenly stopped, because it smelt danger on the road. To this end, Saul alighted, and having smote the ass, it still would not move. Saul then kept on smiting it until it could hardly stand. When Saul lifted up his eyes he beheld a lion standing in his path, and a voice from heaven saying 'Saul, Saul, why persecutest thou me? It is hard for thee to kick against the pricks.'

(No wonder, thought I, that Samuel was grievously disappointed. I am pleased to add that the question was not of my setting.)

A richer vein of amusement to Arthur was provided by the scripts of the eleven-year-old children trying for scholarships to the secondary schools. I have not kept any of these, but remember a few bits that tickled Arthur. The cause of an eclipse of the moon was put down to the sun passing between the earth and the moon. A cat was said to have nine lives, but 'as this is a Christian country they are not required'.

I found it difficult to set any subject for a composition that could not be crammed. Once I tried this: 'You have half an hour to wait in a country railway station. Describe some things you might notice.' One little girl got round this by saying that she would not waste the time in the station but take·a walk in the country. Then followed the purple passage about the birds singing, the sunlight gleaming through the leaves, the brook babbling—and so forth.

'What would you give her for that, Arthur?' I asked.

'Full marks, mother, for being so cunning.'

He was not so sure when I consulted him on another bit of cunning. The subject set was, 'Tell the story that a fir-tree might tell', and the boy candidate told a thrilling detective story.

Oral examinations always followed these written ones; and for this purpose I used to go to various centres in Surrey and Kent, and have a tête-à-tête talk with each child. They could be crammed even for this. For instance, I found it a useful opening sometimes to ask the boy or girl, 'What is your favourite book?' If they obviously were not the reading type, I could get quickly to some other pursuit. One day a little girl replied with ready assurance: 'The Bible.' But when I went on to ask her what she had lately been reading in it, she was dumb. And I soon learnt never to ask anything about poetry, for the child, with fixed eyes, was liable to begin a recitation at once, with due regard to all the prepositions.

Such expeditions were pleasant enough, involving jolly meals and talks with fellow examiners, but I was always glad to come back to the quiet and fresh air of Cuffley.

Some of my fellow examiners came out to see me in this wonderful little spot.

'Is it really true,' was a frequent remark, 'that you can see St. Paul's from here?'

'Yes; hard as it is to believe, we are only fifteen miles from it.'

One day I came home from an inspection with a piece of news. My chief inspector wanted me to write a new Latin book for beginners. If I would make up a story in Latin, he would do the notes on grammar and vocabulary. We agreed that the story must steer between the dreadfully dull and the dreadfully facetious; it must not be a modern story, but must produce the atmosphere of ancient Rome, and bring in real Roman customs, so that learners should not think of the Romans as consisting entirely of soldiers marching about Gaul, demanding hostages.

Fortunately the two elder boys were down from Oxford, and able to give me copious advice. 'Before you start, mother, you must soak yourself in Roman customs,' said one, while the other pulled out the books I was to read. This I set about, and as soon as Arthur and I were alone again, and term had begun, I plotted out all the jolly things three Roman boys could have done, such as seeing a chariot-race, going a coastal sea-voyage, visiting a country farm, and so on. I wanted the grown-ups to have a dinner-party, with some well-known poets as guests. For this purpose, I wrote to my brother Tom, instructing him to write the chapter for me. When the elder boys were at home again, my efforts were severely criticized, any error as to Roman army officials was corrected, and any 'late Latin' word ruthlessly cut out. The book became a family concoction, but Tom's chapter needed no alteration; it leapt to the eye with its easy flow of genuine Latin, as pleasant as a canter after a jog-trot.

Finally I added some easy little Latin plays to the many exercises, and Vivian provided me with a varied feast of bits of English to be put into Latin (providing notes on the idioms).

An old pupil of mine, Violet Gask, was teaching Latin in a large school, and introduced this book to her beginning class. She told them that it had been written by a friend of hers. After a while she had this comment, 'What a funny person Mrs. Hughes must be!' Now whether this was a compliment or the reverse I could not decide. All I know is that it was great fun to write that book, and perhaps some of my fun seeped through.

Another golden gift brought by my work was an inspection in Guernsey, enabling me to see my brother Dym, after an absence of many years. The enormous hug he gave me is a grand memory.

Cuffley was an excellent place for work, but was lacking in any form of recreation. So, during the Oxford vacations, I encouraged Vivian and Barnholt to get holidays away whenever possible. Once they had a mind for a trip to Wales, and I wrote to an old friend at Portmadoc to ask her if she could find some inexpensive rooms for them for a fortnight. She replied that she knew of a reliable man and wife, a worthy couple, who would take them in. She and her husband met them at the station, and then disclosed that they themselves were the 'worthy couple'. I thought this the most charming invitation ever devised. And the whole visit was in accordance with it.

Not so successful was another visit. This time it was the two younger boys—who were invited to stay at the seaside with some friends. Within a week I had a letter from Barnholt asking me if I would write and make some excuse for wanting them *both* to come home. At the end was a scribbled postscript: 'We are coming whether you write or not.' Almost on the top of my getting this letter, the boys appeared. I was curious enough, of course, but made no inquiries, and to this day have only my suspicions to account for that sudden departure.

An Oxford friend of Barnholt's—a frequent dropper-in on us—once expressed to me his idea of home. 'Home,' said he, 'is a place one can stay away from.' He had a specially happy home of his own, and at first his words puzzled me, but on reflection I saw their deeper meaning— that one can stay away and no questions asked. But I think one might add to the definition, 'and is a place one can always come back to'.

In Cuffley itself recreations were almost nil. But one day the local lady had an idea, and came to see me about it.

'I thought,' said she, as soon as seated, 'that it would be a capital plan if we had a little gathering to read something really good—say, some Shakespeare—to read aloud, you know.'

'Yes, but who will gather?'

'Well, besides myself and my daughter there's you and I hope any of your sons who are at home, and some friends of mine from Northaw, and I think I could persuade the Colonel to come.'

'And what play had you in mind for us to murder—not Friends, Romans, Countrymen, I hope?'

'Now, don't talk of murder. I thought of something light, and yet of course good, being Shakespeare. *Twelfth Night*, in fact.'

'That's perhaps the loveliest of the plays, isn't it?'

'Yes, quite, quite. But my chief reason for selecting it is that I happen to have ten paper-covered copies—left over from a reading club.'

'But surely most people here have a copy of Shakespeare?'

'Yes. But in these copies I have pencilled through some questionable words.'

'If you have picked a really light scene with Toby and Aguecheek you must have pencilled through a lot.'

'Not very much; just a word or two here and there.'

We all duly arrived, were given tea in the drawing-room, and then, seated haphazard as we were, received our paper-covered copies and our allotted parts.

Any comic scene, even in current English and on a topical subject, is likely to fall flat in such conditions. But Shakespearian humour, in Elizabethan English, lost its point when read by people too well-bred to put any expression into it. There were no positions taken, no exits or entrances, no gestures. The only funny thing was the caprice of the pencillings; a harmless word (such as 'pregnant', having no indelicate reference) being erased, while other parts that might have brought a blush even to Queen Elizabeth were heavily read.

This meeting began and ended the literary efforts of early Cuffley.

The boys and I culled a fair amount of amusement from the books I had to review. Not that amusement was their aim—far otherwise. We would search the big parcel for anything light and readable, always in vain. Our amusement came when I read aloud fantastic bits from the educational books.

'Whatever can you say about such books, mother?'

'Oh, there's usually something one can praise, if only the print and the paper; and if these are praised the sensible person will know that the book itself is rubbish. Praising the unimportant is just as damning as praising faintly.'

'Yes, but people ought to be warned off the rotten.'

'Of course, sometimes, as in this case.'

'This case' was a book of talks for children in a Sunday school. The teacher, descanting on the goodness of God, was to say that He made the waves on the sea-shore ripple in gently in order that children might paddle. My comment was that the author was obviously not Cornish.

But every parcel brought something of solid worth, often a cheap edition of some standard work, to add to our shelves.

Since our first experience of wireless in old Brand's shed this new form of entertainment had been gaining ground, and had been installed in some of the houses of the *élite* on the Ridgeway. It was to one of these houses that we were all invited to come and spend Christmas afternoon, 'to hear the wireless'. A number of friends and relations assembled in the large drawing-room, and sat round a loud-speaker, all agog to hear this marvel. It started; but to our discomfort it turned out to be some kind of afternoon service. This was a new experience, and we had no idea what to do—to kneel for the prayers, to stand for the hymns, or just to sit solid. We chose the last, each dreading to catch the eye of another. We endured to the end, for it seemed irreverent to turn it off.

When I described our misery to the local lady a few days later, she exclaimed, 'My dear, that's nothing to what I endured the other day. I was invited to dinner, having no idea of this fiendish invention. Just as the fish was being served to me, a voice burst forth from nowhere with "Lord, have mercy upon us". The family had got used to the thing, and went on with their dinner and talk all through prayers and exhortations.'

In another house I was shown into a room where the wireless was working away by itself, for what purpose I could not imagine. With these examples of its use, I took no interest in the invention for a long time.

Whatever the lack of literature and art, a certain amount of real civilization was creeping into Cuffley. An enterprising young man from Cheshunt, named Wackett, brought us daily papers on his bicycle. At first it must have been a precarious livelihood, for some people seemed to think that as papers were so cheap it couldn't matter much whether they were paid for or not. But he throve and still thrives, a general favourite in Cuffley, ever ready to help anyone in distress.

By sheer chance I discovered that there was a kind of shop in Cuffley, lurking among the many outbuildings of the old farm near the station. Here you could 'obtain' sugar, candles, matches, and all those things that one runs out of at critical moments. The place reminded me of a little shop in Cornwall that my mother knew, where a list of articles for sale ended with the words 'mouse-traps and other sweetmeats'.

We heard, too, that at the farm it was possible to telephone: you sat in the little lobby, put down sixpence, and rang up. It sounded nice and private and easy to do. So one day, when I wanted to find out some point about an examination paper, I thought, Why not telephone? The number was clearly stated on the notepaper, almost inviting one to use it. So I knocked at the ever-open farm door, put down my sixpence, and was given a chair near the telephone.

'Number, please,' came with awful suddenness as soon as I rang.

'Seven thousand,' said I, being well rehearsed in it.

'Exchange, please.'

'I have paid my sixpence. I want seven thousand.'

'Exchange, please, we must have the exchange.'

'It's the London University. You must know it.'

'We must have the exchange.' The voice had grown peevish; so, putting it down to some petty officiousness, I replaced the receiver and went home.

Arthur was hugely amused about it when he came home from school, and quietly pointed out to me the 'exchange' on the university notepaper. How do boys always know this kind of thing?

One more bit of civilization had come near us. While

33

our own road remained nameless and in a state of nature, a new one had been laid out at Goff's Oak. It was to be called St. Joan's Road, since Shaw's play had started a vogue for the name. Perhaps the man who had been employed to paint it up was a Welshman, who knew not Joan. Whatever the reason, the name appeared on the board as St. Jones Road, and has remained to be a puzzle for future hagiographers.

Among the relaxations of a social kind in early Cuffley was one for which the neighbourhood was specially suitable —a sketching club. This had been formed by a small coterie of enthusiasts at Northaw, who invited Vivian to join it. Drawing and music were his favourite hobbies, and he had spent much of his spare time at Oxford in either sketching bits of the colleges or in practising with the Bach Choir. At Cuffley his music had to be confined to our own piano, but he eagerly joined in the sketching club. He had already done a great many photographs—amusing mementoes to-day of Cuffley's original simplicity. Studies in colour were quite another business, and the place abounded in picturesque old buildings, such as red-tiled moss-grown old barns, distant views of varying grey and blue, with sunny spots of greenery enfolded among masses of middle-distance trees—all demanding colour and defying the photographer.

The boys discovered, too, a dancing club. Behind our nondescript shop, some distance from the road, was a one-time barn, entitled the Cabin, where teas were served to hikers, school-parties, and mothers on their annual outings. This served as a hall for a dance. There was no distinction of class and a good deal of fun, I gathered. In later years the barn was turned into a brand new hall, still called the Cabin, still used for meetings and dances, but not quite so unconscious of class distinctions.

IV

Religious Activities

NATURALLY I made early inquiries about the church in Cuffley. The Harts, who were devoted church-goers, gave me full information. Our 'metropolitan' was Northaw, the parish church over a mile away (and much farther when weather prevented the use of the field-path). In other directions, and at similar distances, were churches at Newgate Street and Goff's Oak. The little corrugated iron church at Cuffley was a kind of chapel-of-ease for the scattered parishioners of Northaw. It was this last that we found most convenient, since we could reach it in five minutes across the fields.

Not but what we tried them all. Newgate Street was so low in its conduct of the service as to be what the boys called 'crawling'. A very good preacher at Goff's Oak atoned for any other short-comings, and we often went there; but the walk was a long one, when I had the dinner on my mind.

Northaw itself had great attractions. The village, far from a railway, had an almost medieval atmosphere: a village green, a towered church, a picturesque inn, a large vicarage, a national school, a bakery, two small shops, and some cottages. In the background, in stately houses, dwelt some very superior gentry. We had visions of much bowing and scraping, and soup and blankets.

Another medieval touch was the patron saint. Northaw

is one of the very few churches left in England that are under the advocacy of the one really great English saint, Thomas of Canterbury. In old days he was the most popular of all the saints in England until his name was struck off the Calendar by Henry VIII, and his many churches assigned to St. Thomas the Apostle. Perhaps it was the very remoteness of Northaw that led to its saint being overlooked.

One Sunday morning I went over the fields to attend the service. A young clergyman was in charge—presumably a visitor. The ritual was certainly not crawling, and as it chanced to be the feast of the Annunciation, the young preacher chose some appropriate text and began in this strain: 'We all worship God, but how shamefully do we neglect to worship the Mother of God! We pass what we call Lady-day as though it were an ordinary day, and think not at all about that Holy Mother of God.' Here my thoughts wandered, and it struck me what a fine inspiration for mothers that very neglect could be made, an example of self-effacement. I recovered from my reverie to hear the moral of his sermon, which was simply this: we must come to church more often. This sermon discouraged me from ever attending the church again.

Our little corrugated iron church was managed almost entirely by a lay reader, who lived in an adjoining bunga-low. The Vicar of Northaw came over twice a month, either to take the Communion Service or to preach at Matins. I found myself one morning at the Communion Service, forming one of three—the legal limit. The other two were the faithful lay reader and the equally faithful bell-ringer. She was our oldest inhabitant—the mother of the *Plough* Inn. The Vicar began, and the lay reader did the Amens and other responses. During the recital of the Commandments my mind wandered, and I was returned to my surroundings by a strange silence—almost as awakening as a sudden noise. One of the longer commandments had met with no response. The lay reader had fallen asleep, and the old bell-ringer would not presume to take it upon her to interfere. The Vicar waited, and I hesitated. Then came a hurried prayer for mercy from the awakened lay reader, and the hitch was safely over.

That good old lay reader did his best, and had the saving grace of sincerity. His chief duty of course was reading, and that was what he couldn't do. He managed to deprive the lessons, the prayers, the sermons (evidently another's) of their meaning, by heavily emphasizing the wrong words. For instance, the beautiful prayer of St. Chrysostom was made almost ridiculous by his way of coming thump down on the word 'them'.

In the midst of a conference about an examination paper in religious subjects, my fellow examiner was deploring the lack of candidates for the section on the Prayer Book, and the ignorance of it in the world at large. 'Why,' said he, 'don't you give a course of lectures in your district on the Revision of the Prayer Book?' He was a humourless man, or I should have misquoted *David Copperfield* and begged him to step out and look at my district. As it was I closed his mouth by saying that most of the people in my neighbourhood did not know so much as whether there *be* a Prayer Book.

In due course our Vicar paid a call on me, and I found

him a delightful fellow, with a keen sense of the ridiculous. He knew well enough what we were suffering from the lay reader, so (apropos of the small attendance at church) I amused him with my mother's story of her Cornish Vicar, who, seeing his one-man audience, began Evensong once in this way: 'Dearly beloved Rogers.'

'His sermons have become more than I can endure,' said I, 'so I slip out just before he begins, look as ill as I can, and tell people that I suffer from logophobia—that's why I sit at the back. They are too delicate to inquire further into the disease. I hope this rumour will reach the lay reader, for I wouldn't hurt his feelings on any account; he works hard I'm sure.'

'Yes, I believe he labours heavily over those alien sermons.'

'Why don't you induce him,' said I, 'to tell us about something he has come across during the week, at his business or in travelling—someone injured and taken care of—any bit of kindness he has noticed?'

'Ah!' broke in the Vicar. 'He couldn't! What you suggest sounds so simple, but it's really the most difficult thing in the world. Our Lord's teaching was entirely on these lines, but it isn't a bow for every man to shoot with.'

'I suppose the trouble must always lie in the different needs of the congregation. As a friend of mine says, "I don't want to be *always* preaching for tired old women".'

'You would be surprised,' said the Vicar, 'at the oddities we get in Cuffley. I touched bottom when I first came here: I was paying a call in this part, and the daughter of the house said to me, "I wish you would tell me who this Jesus Christ was that they talk about".'

'No,' said I, 'it doesn't surprise me. I have seen too much of religious instruction in schools to be surprised at her ignorance of the New Testament. They seem to batten on Old Testament stories and learning Psalms by heart.'

'Exactly. And are bored into complete indifference.'

'There's no lack of faith, though, of the "fundamental" type. You know our dear old schoolmistress here? Well, I happened to be in the train with her the other day, and she was telling me of a nephew who had been in the Garden of Eden during the war, and had brought her a leaf of the tree of Knowledge. "How interesting!" I exclaimed. "Do tell me what kind of tree it was; I've always wanted to know." To which she replied in shocked tones, "It was *the* Tree."'

We had a good laugh over this, but agreed that it was no laughing matter, for Old Testament theology can do so much harm.

As an illustration of this I may add that once I was travelling on our line and fell into talk with a woman. She was so religious-minded that she felt 'guided' continually; and at the moment was full of a terrible case: a man in Aylesbury had become a Communist, and the very next day he had been *crushed to pieces* by a lorry. The inference was so clear that the Almighty had been annoyed at the young man's turn of thought, that I felt obliged to lodge a protest.

'But after all, there's nothing *wicked* about Communism. Our Lord himself was a Communist, wasn't he?'

'Eh, yes. But very soon the Church found that it wouldn't work—wasn't practical.'

'Quite,' said I, and added, 'What a pity it is that he was so ignorant of the possibilities of the world he wanted to save. Or,' I added dreamily, 'was he?'

She got out at the next station. I fancy she must have belonged to some peculiar sect, for our neighbourhood has never lacked variety of creed. It was a nonconformist minister of Cuffley who ascribed to the Almighty quite another 'act of God' motive. A daring and often naughty small boy met with a bad accident when bicycling, and the minister called to inquire for him, obviously expecting the worst and prepared no doubt to point the moral. But the boy was getting better, and ideas had to be readjusted. 'I know,' said he, 'why his life has been preserved; he is not yet fit to die; his soul is not yet saved.' It leaps to the mind that such a theology is a direct incentive to naughtiness.

In looking back on that visit of our Vicar, I am more and more convinced that he was right when he said, 'Believe me, I have far less trouble in teaching anyone who is frankly ignorant about our Lord, than in dealing with the many folk about here who know all about the intentions of Providence, but are offended at the opinions of their Master when translated from the Authorized Version into modern English.'

One incident during our early days in Cuffley stands out vividly in my memory. It is a companion picture to my experience of the awkward hitch in the Ten Commandments. On just such another Sunday morning I found myself one of a congregation of about a dozen. Instead of the Vicar, a visiting clergyman, a youngish man, appeared. I have attended countless Communion Services, of every description, from the highly ornate and choral to the

41

severely simple. But never have I known one so impressive as that. The Ten Commandments gave place to the Two. Everything was read as if fresh-minted. There was no trace of over-expression or 'feeling', but the man seemed to be meaning every word he uttered, and a long experience tells me that this cannot be put on. I have no idea who this man was, nor what his doctrine may have been about the real presence, but it was the first and only time that I have felt the spirit of it.

As time went on the story of our little iron church has been chequered by several changes of clergymen from Northaw, while our faithful lay reader carried on steadily with his work. The congregation was never large, and he explained this to one of the boys as being due to 'a wave of indifference sweeping over the country'. The metaphor tickled us, nor did we believe in the statement it set forth. Not indifference, but irritation, was the cause of my own falling off, for one.

A church can never be too plain and simple in its appointments; it is decoration that distracts. On every spare space of wall was hung one of those all too familiar Sunday school pictures of our Lord depicted as a sentimental dispenser of sweet thoughts and deeds, with picturesque Eastern peasants in convenient attitudes around. If, like the Ancient Mariner, I turned my eyes away, they would fall on the lectern cloth, which was a vivid bilious green. If I shut my eyes and kept them closed, I fell asleep.

All such trifles could be put up with; but at last there was another trouble that proved too much for me. There chanced to arrive in Cuffley a new parishioner, who began to prove a thorn in the flesh to our lay reader. He was one of those ostentatiously religious laymen, who seem to annoy ordinary people as much as they annoyed our Lord. He knew all the things that a parson ought to do in the conduct of a service, and also what the congregation ought to do—when to say *Amen* and when to refrain, when to stand and when to kneel—and a lot more of these minutiae, hitherto unknown to the lay reader. All such details would have been welcomed if imparted in a smiling spirit of *bonhomie* over a cup of coffee in the layman's house, or even over a pint of beer in the *Plough*. But the new parishioner never appeared to smile or look jolly about anything, and unfortunately the lay reader was not decently grateful when his delinquencies were pointed out to him. We all knew how hard he had worked to keep any congregation at all, and to do his best for the simple folk from the outlying farms, and we guessed how he must resent being fussed about things that mattered not a jot.

So when we had to see this newcomer walking along with his palms together, kneeling down at certain clauses in the Creed (when the rest of us thought standing was good), and always looking unhappy, we found it a worse thing to bear than the pictures or the lectern cloth. However, the lay reader carried on bravely for many years, until his work, or better (or worse) fortune, caused him to leave Cuffley. He died very soon afterwards, always fretting at having to leave his work in our little iron church. We cannot pass it without thinking of him gratefully.

V

A New Venture

THE year 1922 brought stirrings among our eight little
houses. The Harts had outgrown their quarters and
gone away, being well enough off to buy a large house.
Money had also apparently come to the mother of my
bicycle-instructor.

'We are leaving Cuffley,' said she to me one morning.

'Oh? Where are you going?' idly I replied.

'To a certain distance,' said she, in a tone of closure.

Horrified at my supposed curiosity, and concluding that
at least her husband had been given some post in the Foreign
Office, I could only murmur how pleasant it was to be
certain about the distance, and then took refuge in the
weather. (They had taken a house in Enfield.)

Taking a house, during those four or five years after the
War, was an event. An empty house was almost unknown,
and no sooner had our enriched neighbours made their
hegira to Enfield, than there were new-comers in their place.

'I think they must be *nouveaux riches*, mother,' said
Vivian one day, looking out of the window, 'the wife is
wearing a fur coat.'

A fur coat can be very telling. A young friend of mine
tried in vain to get a job, although she was well qualified;
in despair she spent her substance on a fur coat, and obtained a job at once.

However, in this case, the fur coat told anything but the

truth. Our new-comers, to whom we extended neighbourly smiles and so on, told us the curious chance that had forced them to find any kind of temporary shelter in Cuffley. The owner of the land on one side of the Ridgeway, including the extensive wood, had bought it with the idea of making a 'Garden Estate'. For this purpose he had engaged the services of our new neighbour, Mr. K., an architect-builder, to plan and supervise the whole scheme. This was particularly welcome because the War had deprived Mr. K. of his usual building work. But, to his bitter disappointment, the whole thing stopped. Five days after his arrival in Cuffley, the landowner died, and Mr. K. was left high and dry. Whether owing to internecine family war, or to lack of enterprise, I can't say, but the business plan was still-born.

Mr. K. had done some of the planning work, and sent in his small bill for it. No notice was taken. He sent it in again, and again. Then he set his teeth and swore that he would not leave Cuffley till he got it. (It has never come, and Mr. K. is still in Cuffley—going strong as its leading builder.)

How I wished that I could get Mr. K. to build a house for us. The boys were getting too big to have to sleep in one room; they were so much of a size that they used to say, 'The best-dressed is the one who gets up first.' But my restricted means forbade my dreaming of providing better quarters anywhere, let alone building.

Then we discovered that our semi-detached neighbours were contemplating such an adventure. The lay reader had built himself a bungalow next to the church. Now whether it was to add to his slender congregation or to his slender means, one can but guess: on the strength of having built a bungalow, he offered to build a house for our neighbours. I think a bungalow must be easier to build than a house— anyhow this new house seemed awkwarder and awkwarder as it rose . . . the lay reader was no architect.

Mrs. Semi-detached was thrilled at the prospect of be- coming one of the superior people on the Ridgeway. But there was a fly in the ointment.

'I am so afraid,' she said to me, 'that being so close to the church we shall have no excuse for being absent from the services. And what if my husband should become religious?'

'But is that anything to worry about?'

'I've heard of people being taken that way . . . a relation of ours was . . . most unhappy . . . .'

I didn't like to inquire into such sinister consequences, but gave it as my opinion that her husband would be safe enough, as long as he abstained from week-day services. She took this quite seriously. As it happened all went well, and this hard-headed bank-clerk never developed religious mania.

Meanwhile Mr. K. had not been idle. He found that a piece of land a little farther along the Ridgeway could be bought at a reasonable price, and on the mere chance of getting some building work to do, had invested in it. When I heard about it, I exclaimed to Mrs. K.,

'Why, that's where people get murdered, isn't it?'

'Well, it's next to the farm, but that needn't happen again.'

Old Castle Farm on the Ridgeway had been in the care of a man and his wife, who saw to the sheep-rearing and sundry crops. It was a lonely spot, and the dullness had no doubt got on the man's nerves; he attempted to murder his wife and then committed suicide. An actual suicide never seems to me so terrible as the thought of the state of mind that made it inevitable.

Mrs. K. and I went up to have a look at the piece of ground. It was entirely overgrown with brambles and a miserable kind of willow-tree, interspersed with a few oaks. But it was high ground with fine views, and we could easily picture the joys of a house on it.

At this tide in our affairs I was left a legacy of £300 by my old friend Miss M. J. Busk. I wish she could know what a godsend it was. I had managed to save a little money, and I knew I could sell our small house, and now with this addition it was like flying in the face of Providence not to launch forth into building one for ourselves. The boys were all for it: Vivian thought I might venture; Barnholt said it was no use worrying about the future—a man who knew what he would be doing next year was already an old man; Arthur was always game for anything.

With this weight of opinion behind me I asked Mr. K. to come in one evening and talk over possibilities.

'Now what do you want in the way of rooms for your house?' was his first question as he fingered his paper and pencil.

'One big room, where all four of us can stretch and be untidy; a bedroom, however small, for each of us; and these must be upstairs; a small kitchen, and a bathroom.'

'Right,' he replied, already making rough sketches; 'I'll come in when I have made a plan and an estimate, to discuss it with you.'

'I think,' said he, 'that I can manage a small second sitting-room on the ground floor.'

After this his visits were daily and often hourly. We had to discuss which side of the kitchen was best for the gas-stove, where the front door should be, what should be the aspect of the big room, and what spaces should be allowed for the larger pieces of furniture.

This last point seems unimportant, but to me it meant a great deal. My husband and I had always dreamt of building a house some day. And here I was, doing it without him—the whole point knocked away. But I hoped to make it breathe the spirit of his old home in Wales. Together we had collected some old oak furniture—a Welsh dresser from an inn at Aberdovey, and a 'cubbard dyddarn' (a large double cupboard) that we found in a cottage hardly bigger than the cupboard itself. There was the old walnut table round which his family had had their meals, and there was the grand old clock made for his father by Henry Owen of Caernarvon (depicting not only the usual full moon and shipwreck, but also a realistic painting of Daniel in the lions' den). It was this grandfather clock that required the big room to be eight feet high. And spaces of about six feet were needed for the pieces of Welsh furniture and the piano. As for aspect, I wanted as much sun as I could get.

Mr. K. was obviously delighted to be at his own work again, for the War had put a stop to everything of the kind, and this house of ours was to be his first act of renewal. It seemed to me just the atmosphere for the building of our home that my husband would rejoice in.

Much of Mr. K.'s talk was quite beyond me, but I tried to look intelligent as he talked of 'three by twos', 'rabbets' at a door-step, 'tread and rise', and all the comparative advantages and prices. But now and again I lodged a protest.

'Space between the bricks! Hollow walls!' I exclaimed. 'Won't the money run to solid walls?'

Laughter greeted this. 'Why, hollow walls are more expensive, but well worth the money; you see, warm air circulates round the house, like a blanket, keeping it from cold and damp.'

One remark of his did certainly alarm me. He intended, so he said with pride, to build the house upon a raft. I had a vision of our all floating away some day, like the people in *Rudder Grange*. But the raft was to be made of concrete, and defy all tricks of soil and weather. I still think it a most misleading name for a foundation.

When the final layout of the house was shown me, I saw how useful that second little sitting-room would be, not only as a city of refuge for work, but also as a place to stow our overflowing books. At a sale years before my husband had picked up a section of the library of Lord Chesterfield, part of the bookcase that had gone round the room; I saw that this could now be properly housed, and the little room be devoted to books.

There followed pleasant discussions about leaded lights, the design for the chimney, oven-tiles for the kitchen (so easily washed), parquet flooring for the downstairs rooms (avoiding any need for a carpet), the make of tile for the roof. Mr. K. came in so often about these details, that Mrs. K. told me with great amusement how Cuffley had raised an eyebrow about it.

'Well,' said I, 'if Cuffley thinks that I can carry on a clandestine flirtation with a rather deaf man in an open window, and go for walks daily with his wife as well, they must be very hard up for a subject of conversation.'

Hardly a day passed without our going to see the 'site'. Workmen had already begun to make a clearance through the tangle, so that a cart could be driven in; and soon the time came for me to choose which portion of the plot I preferred, for there was enough ground for two houses. I decided on the part remote from the road, which gave an uninterrupted view over beautiful undulating country towards the south-east. This portion included some good oak-trees and a small pond. The path already cut would serve as a drive from the road to the house. The plot staked out for me was about half an acre.

Then the raft was laid and the house begun. Mr. K. brooded over every operation. Once, I remember, he made the men take down their work on the wall of the projecting bow-window, and do it all over again. It was in these early stages that Arthur and I were allowed each to lay a brick, and inscribe our names on them. The elder boys were away, or we should all have 'had a hand' in building the house.

And someone else had a hand. Mr. K. belonged to a well-known family of architects in Dorset, and his father became greatly interested in his son's new venture in Cuffley.

On the feeble pretext that I had shown kindness to Mrs. K., he offered to design a mantelpiece for our big room. And a noble design it has proved: carried out in local Hertfordshire oak, it looks like part of the house, and provides two ever-blessed side projections—one for smoking appurtenances, the other for letters that *must* be attended to.

No pains were spared by Mr. K. to find other pieces of oak for window-sills, supports for the veranda, and overbeams for the bow-windows. One of these came from a Hertfordshire brewery, and looks as old as Shakespeare (perhaps it is).

At last the roof was finished, tiles and all. I think that building a house must be something like making a dress—when it is put together and become a 'dress', the long tiresome work begins with the finishings. But I did not know that fact in 1923, when in early July Mr. K. told me that there were 'only the finishings' to be done.

'Can you give me a date?' said I, 'because the people who have bought our present house have written to know when they can come in.'

He thereupon named a date when the new house would be ready for occupation, and may the Lord have mercy upon his soul.

On receiving this information, I passed on the date to the inquiring new-comers, and also got hold of a local man who could bring a lorry to move our furniture up the hill. He came, gave a glance round, named his charge, and took a note of the date for the job.

During the next ten days or so the boys and I spent every minute we could spare from our work in packing clothes into trunks, books into orderly batches, and china into well-wrapped bundles. We were too busy to go up the hill to look at the house.

Anybody who has ever moved will agree that the most unaccommodating objects are books. Their subjects bear no relation to their size and shape. They are too heavy to be carried in their cases. They never fit into any wooden box. While you are labouring at tying them into bundles with string so that they shall not slither out, they lie about everywhere, their number somehow multiplied by a hundred. Seeing me in despair over them, Barnholt exclaimed,

'I've got an idea, mother. I'll collect all those you haven't strung together, and put them in the bath till to-morrow. You are too tired for more to-night, and to-morrow I'll bring you plenty of string and you can sit by the bath and finish them.'

'But suppose water gets to them?'

'My dear mother, don't be silly; you know the trouble we have with those taps to get a bath at all.'

I could but agree, and he spent an hour or two putting into the bath all the books he could find lying about. With the devilry that possesses inanimate objects, one of those taps chose to dribble during the night, and to this day some of my most cherished editions bear the watermarks of those hours. I am sure some learned person would be able to assign a reason for the disaster—a coming change in the weather, moisture in the air after a long drought, or something equally convincing. But we were all in such high spirits that we could only laugh. Each boy was going to have a room to himself, and there are few acquisitions in life more satisfying.

To celebrate the day of our new life, Barnholt managed to acquire a huge basket of strawberries, and he put them in my hands triumphantly. One remembers for ever some special gifts.

VI

Settling In

A NOTHER bit of experience I pass on to those as foolish as myself. The man who comes to make what he calls an estimate for removing goods, is apparently pressed for time, since his reason for charging nearly double his estimate turns out to be ignorance of the amount of stuff there was to move. You may say, 'Well, keep him to his word, pay him no more than his estimate.' That sounds business-like. But he has a way of disclosing his amazement at the amount to be shifted *before* he has unloaded it. Now we are all human, and the evil spirits of unlawful acquisition, or even vengeance, may get the better of him. If anyone during the misery of a move can be 'all there' enough to check everything she possesses, I have yet to meet her. I say 'her', because the ordinary man is not such easy prey.

The best of a big worry is that it drives out all the little ones. My annoyance at being overcharged for the removal soon gave way to my dismay at the state of our new home. Of course I had reckoned on our removing-workmen to put most of the furniture in position. But the parquet-flooring of the big room had not been begun. The wooden bricks were occupying the floor in piles. Not a single thing could be placed there. So our piano and Chesterfield-couch, our Welsh cupboard and dresser, oak chest and chairs, all had to be dumped in the garden.

The next revelation was that there were no stairs. A nice

big 'well' was there, but not the ghost of a stair. A ladder
was propped up for our use in the manner of Jacob's dream,
and the beds were hoisted up the well by means of ropes.
So, at all events, thought I, there will be somewhere to
sleep.

There was also a vast wardrobe that they managed to
hoist up. We used it as a wardrobe, but it had none of the
appearance of such a thing. It may have been built to ac-
commodate deeds and other law-papers, as its history
suggests. It was discovered in the underground region of
my husband's chambers at No. 1 Hare Court. No one
knew anything about it, and the other barristers in the
building suggested that he, as a family man, might find it
useful in his home. We certainly found it useful, for it
proved a grand container of everything one needs to put
on, and still there is room. It has no pretence to ornament,
but is made of some strong, polished, unspecified wood,
and contains reliable shelves and one deep drawer. I have
often wondered what its future will be, for it will never be
possible to bring it down by way of the stairs, nor can it
be got through the casement windows. It reminds me of a
cottage I saw in Wales where an enormous four-poster bed
filled up almost the entire room. When I asked how it got
in, they told me it had been made inside.

Another heavy article hoisted up the well was a solid oak
chest, covered with camel-hair, that was used by my Cornish
uncle when a schoolboy a hundred years ago, and still bears
inside the lid the list of his clothes, from nine shirts to three
silk handkerchiefs and forks and spoons—all in the careful
handwriting of his mother.

The third unhappy situation we had to face was the lack of plumbing. Water was to be had, because no builders can get on without it. But of sanitary arrangements there was no trace.

To counterbalance these drawbacks, we were all full of high spirits about our adventure, and the weather was superb. It was one of those rare summers in England when for weeks on end one almost forgets the existence of rain and clouds. We could easily picnic for a few days.

That very same night we had the worst thunderstorm that had been known for years. We dreaded to look at the damage done to our furniture in the garden. It has all recovered now from that torrent of rain, but it took an extremely long time—years, in fact.

Our misfortunes led Mr. K. to put his own hand to the laying down of the parquet-flooring, and before the week was out the poor pieces of furniture were placed in the positions planned so carefully for them. And they have not stirred since, while the couch and chairs and tables are constantly on the move, to suit our own whims. I made what I thought an excellent rule about this big room: no books to be kept in it. To a certain extent the rule was obeyed; no books were *kept* in it, but they were continually seeping in, and making a temporary lodging on chairs, stools, and floor. And as few things in this room were ever where they ought to be, the boys dubbed it 'the big shambles'. The little room was to be devoted to the books, which were housed there after each boy had carted his own special books to his bedroom to put in his own bookcase. I soon found that the Chesterfield case would only hold half of the quantity we had; so after a few weeks I asked Mr. K. to put up for us some deal shelves against one wall from floor to ceiling. Books are very tiresome to arrange, with their different heights, and I had to be content with this rough classification: serious books in the Chesterfield; frivolity in the deal.

It has struck me that the prevalence of bungalows must be due to the difficulty of making staircases. We hear of people (sillier even than those who make their own wills) who make their own plans for their houses, only to find that they have forgotten the stairs. One's mind doesn't dwell on the stairs any more than one's body does.

Now of course Mr. K. hadn't forgotten the stairs, for the well was there. But days passed with nothing done. He would come and gaze at the well, and make notes in pencil on the palm of his left hand (an ever-ready memorandum book); then he would go away to contemplate them in private.

During this Mahomet's-coffin period, my brother Tom walked in one day. He had come from Yorkshire to see how we were getting on.

'I hope you don't mind being without any stairs,' said I, as I pointed to the ladder.

'Rather not!' said he. 'Why, it's just like lake-dwelling—so safe at nights from rats and burglars.'

Nothing had ever been known to disturb Tom, and he joined in all our picnic ways like a schoolboy. We went for long walks through woods and fields, across brooks and along such lanes as Tom thought were only to be found in Devon. Lerry leapt along by our side—another joy to

Tom after the restricted life of the streets of Middlesbrough.

And the big shambles amused him too, with its no silly fuss about muddy shoes or tobacco ash, and its lack of ornaments.

'Fancy your still keeping that old work-basket, Molly!'

My intimate friends all knew this work-basket; it was the top half of the Japanese basket that had served me on my honeymoon; into it I had been accustomed to thrust everything that wanted mending; then I would bring it out when a friend came, and allow her to help me with the work. 'I can't sew alone,' would be my excuse, 'because I keep on thinking of all the other things I would rather be doing.' Then my friend (whether truthfully or in a Christian spirit I did not seek to know) would say, 'I love sewing; let me do it *all* while we talk.' That so-called work-basket makes me think of the Temple of Janus—only twice in its career has it been emptied of its contents, with all the mending done. The first time was just before my second boy was born, in case I died and left the basket in its disgraceful state. The second time I emptied it under the aegis of a reforming visitor, my old schoolfellow, Bessie Jones.

'How are you going to manage the ordinary household work?' was a question from Tom. 'It was all very well in that tiny place below, said he, 'but up here there will be a good deal more to do.'

'Manage,' said I, 'is too grand a word for what we do— rub along is a better description. The boys are always good at going to fetch things, making their own beds, and even washing up. And after all, I am alone for long stretches of time, when Vivian and Barnholt are at Oxford, and Arthur is at school all day, so there is not much wear and tear or meal-getting.'

'Couldn't you get what they call a "woman in"?' suggested Tom.

'That expression always makes me think of Mary Wood's old cook, who used to say she didn't 'old with wimmin,' said I.

'That about sums up what Nell used to feel. I remember how incensed she was with one woman who was continually cadging. "She would cadge the chair I'm sitting on —I would rather have to deal with an honest-to-goodness thief." '

'Nell must have had some Irish ancestor,' said I, to which Tom heartily agreed.

'As for the ordinary servant in the house, Tom, my experience has been either that they are young and you have to look after their health and their morals; or that they are old, faithful, and blameless and at last boss you entirely. And it's so hard to get rid of a saint.'

'I agree,' said Tom, 'but I don't like your living quite alone if all the boys happen to be away. This house is so far from the road, and even from the nearest neighbours. Won't you be nervous at night?'

'Not a bit,' said I, 'distance and obscurity are positive advantages. The casual thief won't care to navigate our twisty little drive in the dark, and if he did Lerry would soon put the fear of God into him; and as for the accomplished burglar, I've the best proof against him—a complete absence of anything to tempt him.'

'And you don't just feel lonely?'

'No time for that, with heaps to do and friends dropping in at odd times. And having you here, dear old boy, is brave and good as the Cornish say. Haven't you brought me any funny stories this time?'

'Not much. There's one thing I heard—"not sunny but pecoola" as you used to say when you were tiny. A nonconformist man I know begged me to come to his wedding, and I could hardly refuse, much as I dislike these nonconformist services. Of course there had to be that dreadful ordeal—a prayer from the bosom, and believe me it began, "O Lord, Thou knowest this young couple very well".'

'We must hand it to nonconformity for intimacy with the Almighty,' said I, 'but for sheer ignorance our young curates are hard to beat. Bessie Jones was telling me of a sermon she heard the other day when on holiday in some country spot (very remote, I gathered). The text was, "As far as the east is from the west, so far hath he removed our transgressions from us." '

'A fine subject,' said Tom, 'it makes me think of what mother used to say about the clause in the Creed: "I can believe in the forgiveness of other people's sins, but it is myself that I can never forgive." I guess this young man didn't touch on *that* problem, but probably drivelled at length on how comfortable everything would be for us?'

'Yes, and Bessie was only following it with half her mind, when she was stung into attention by this statement: "Our sins are put away for ever beyond our ken—as far as the east is from the west. Our ken, our knowledge. Now we *know* how far the north is from the south for the distance between the north pole and the south pole has been accurately measured. But no one has the least idea of the distance of the east from the west." Bessie would have concluded that he had unearthed some early sixteenth-century homily, if he hadn't shown acquaintance with the discovery of the poles.'

'Why, he could have made a better do,' said Tom, 'if he had expatiated on the oddity of the lost day when we cross the Atlantic. It would have interested any congregation, and have a smack of the mysterious about it, without which, I fear, no sermon is successful!'

'Yes,' said I. 'Isn't it Wells who wrote somewhere that most people will always prefer a wonder story to a moral effort?'

'And I expect the net result of all this measureless distance was just the same as most sermons—a variation of the theme "Comfort ye my people".'

'Mind you, Tom, teaching hath her oddities no less renowned than preaching. You should hear some of the Latin lessons I endure.'

'Quantities bad with the women teachers?'

'Not so much bad, as non-existent, *when* the text is read; many lessons have no reading in Latin at all, but frequent rehearsal of tenses like this: "monybam, monybas, monybat". As a rule I leave all criticism till a private talk, but sometimes I feel obliged to protest then and there. I attended a class of beginners in Latin who were having a lesson on early Rome. No map, or other indication of where in the world Rome was, but a pretty story of Romulus and Remus. When Remus not only jumped over the wall, but went on to slay Romulus, I quietly said, "I think you meant the other way, didn't you? Wasn't it Romulus who slew Remus?" "Oh, no," said the teacher brightly, "it was Remus who slew Romulus; it says so in this little book." "How odd!" said I. "Let me see it", and I was handed *Glimpses into Ancient Lands*, or some such title.'

'I know the sort of book,' said Tom, 'and sha'n't be surprised to hear that it slaughtered Romulus.'

'Oh no, it was correct enough; the teacher admitted she had made a slip and proceeded with her lesson quite happily, thinking no doubt that I was a university fusspot.'

'The boys must enjoy the stories you bring home,' said Tom.

'They are generally too busy with their own work to listen; but one thing they love more than anything else came from my days at Whitelands, where I discovered that the slogan in their practising schools appeared to be "Hands away! All eyes on me!" '

'I suppose the distracted teachers with sixty children can do no more than keep them in order.'

'Just that. In spite of Montessori and Dalton methods, and every kind of effort by Whitelands and the other training colleges, the "Hands away" period is bound to prevail as long as any one person has to teach sixty wriggling bits of humanity at once.'

'Our noble Ministers of Education have probably never in their lives entered the portals of an elementary school. I should like to rub their noses in a few of them.'

'Yes. I wished once that Someone in Authority could have been with me. It fell to my duty to take half a dozen students from Whitelands to hear a "model lesson" from a leading teacher in an elementary school. It was on Richard I, and the lesson went quite brightly. Then the teacher said, "Take down these questions: 1. Name three places where Richard went, and say what he did in each. 2. What do you think of the character of Richard as a king?" '

'That sounds pretty good,' said Tom.

'Exactly. So the students and I thought, to judge by our smiles of appreciation on one another while the questions were being taken down. But imagine our amazement when this was followed by the teacher's saying, "I will now dictate the answers." '

'Whatever did you say to the students about it?'

'Only the stark reality—that if one had to correct sixty papers, one could do no more than see to writing and spelling. But as a *model* lesson!'

Tom never saw our stairs; but before he left he had a good idea of the new home, which we called Fronwen, after the old family house in Wales. We were all sorry for Tom to go. He was a delightful man to have 'about the house'. He was always at home in any company that he chanced upon, and always on the spot in any domestic emergency or everyday needs. Any deprivation was a joke rather than a nuisance. 'Looking dismal gets you nowhere,' he would say, and immediately get somewhere. In contrast to his practical side, he was endowed by nature with a magnificent laziness of demeanour, which was in itself a poultice. I think his education at Shrewsbury must have been a fine one; for he always preferred the enjoyment of good literature and a fierce game of cricket to any effort

after worldly advancement. He lost several headmaster-
ships by not stating his qualifications properly, and in one
case by missing the train for the final interview. But the
loss didn't trouble him. This kind of thing happened so
often that I have a shrewd idea that subconsciously he preferred to remain where he was—not well off in worldly
goods, but in friends a millionaire. His son, in sending me
some memories of his father, described how one day (when
close on sixty) he sauntered up to a tram-stop only to see
that it had started and was some twenty yards ahead. He
then darted after it, caught and boarded it while it was
going. This little incident seems like a picture of his whole
life.

It was partly the fun of having Tom with us, and partly
the confusion of settling in to our new quarters—whatever
the reason—I had actually forgotten to send off a batch of
examination scripts. A note reminding me that they were
wanted at my earliest convenience gave me a turn. Always
ahead with my work, I had duly marked these scripts, made
the list, and written the report. But where had I put the
parcel? It was not a large one, and might be anywhere.
Of course it ought to have been in my 'University drawer',
but drawers had all been emptied for the removal, and removers have a genius for putting things in odd places.
Casting all other jobs aside, I began with my mother's
invariable precepts: 1. It can't be underground; 2. Where
did you have it last? This second slogan we used to call
the historical method, but was no use in a move. Then I
tried discarding the places where it couldn't be, such as the
piano and the grandfather clock—the method of elimina-

tion, which Arthur, when a small boy, used to call the method of illumination. Then I tried my final effort, the small-tooth-comb method. Determined to search the whole house without regard to order, I started on a mixed pile of music, pictures, and tablecloths. 'Every inch,' I cried savagely, and in a few minutes there were the scripts, at the bottom of the pile.

So things were getting right at last; not only were the stairs put in, but the plumbers had finished their job. I suspect that even Mr. K. himself is subservient to his plumber, who is everywhere an autocrat. And why? Because he puts the pipes in, and knows *where they are*. When they burst, not even Tom can cope with them. You are forced to have what an old lady friend of mine used to call 'a proper man' to mend them—in other words, a plumber. The dark suspicion occurs to the mind that these men place the pipes in the most awkward positions so that none but one of the brotherhood can find them. For instance, this winter, water began to pour forth in Arthur's bedroom—a new place. So I sent for Bill (that is really his name). Bill contemplated the disaster for some time in silence, and then said that the mischief lay between the roof and the ceiling of Arthur's room, and to reach this he would have to take down part of the wall of the bathroom and creep in from there. I retired, a bit awe-struck.

After about two hours, Bill reappeared with the words: 'It's all right now, mum, and I've made good.'

Yes, the bathroom looked as before, and Arthur's ceiling looked as if butter wouldn't melt in its mouth.

'But how did you manage to get in?' I asked.

'Bit of a squeeze, it was. All right getting in, it's the wriggling back that's the job. You see, I was in a submarine in the last war, and we had to make ourselves small. I remember one chap who got into a place and couldn't get back—not for a long time.'

I shuddered at the possibility of having a plumber in my roof for an indefinite period. It was a new light on nature that it is easier to wriggle forward than backward, and I had visions of the poor fellow having to wait till lack of food made him smaller, like the fox in the barn.

Is it any wonder that a plumber ranks high among our national jokes? For these always deal with some dire and ineluctable misfortune, classed together as 'scaffold jokes'.

Lack of stairs, presence of plumbers, loss of my papers— these were among the major worries of our new life. But there was one little annoyance that enraged me more than any of them. The people who had bought our old house down below had clamoured to have it ready for their occupation on a given date, and we pushed ahead with our move so as not to disappoint them. Imagine then my disgust when they didn't arrive till a week later!

VII

New Neighbours

As soon as the builders had cleared their things away (a long process) we began on the garden. One point we were all agreed upon—it must not be a suburban affair, with quaintly shaped beds, and flowers carefully arranged as to colour, not to speak of sun-dials, bird-baths, plaster rabbits, and gnomes. A small plot was set aside for vegetables, and for the rest we determined on plenty of grass and trees, confining the flowers to borders, where they could push their way cottage-fashion.

A beginning was made with the score of fruit-trees (apples, pears, and plums) that we had planted in the former garden and had brought up with us. And we had some rose-trees of my husband's planting that had gone with me everywhere. I bought a few foot-high Scotch firs, and in the woods we found plenty of young birches, from which we selected some for ourselves. Rowans and various creepers were either bought or presented, seeds and small plants gave us plenty of flowers, and in time the garden began to take shape, or rather refused to take shape, but had its points of interest from its very shapelessness.

The chief interest for children is a path that I specially insisted on. With varying levels, involving steps here and there, and with seductive side-issues, it runs right round the whole garden. It is where this path gets higher along the south-east hedge that grown-ups find another interest—

a sight of the dome of St. Paul's, and the glorious 'green belt' between. It is this view of St. Paul's that enables us to claim to be Londoners still. My own favourite bit is what we call the 'dimble', an untidy part, sheltered by oaks, where we burn the garden rubbish, and can take cover if undesirable visitors are seen approaching the house. Arthur, as my youngest son, has naturally been at home longer than the others, and has taken special interest in making the garden. Even now, on his rare visits, almost his first words are, 'Come on, mother, let's go round and examine the agricultural outlook.'

But dearer to him than even the garden was the shed. This is a roomy tiled outhouse, built by Mr. K. before he began the actual house, chiefly, I fancy, for his own private ends. It contained a carpenter's bench, a place for coal, and could harbour bicycles and anything else. 'The very thing, mother,' said Arthur, 'for my chemistry experiments.'

It chanced that one of Arthur's schoolfellows, a boy distinguished on the science side at Merchant Taylors', was taken suddenly ill and died. His grief-stricken father acted very wisely about his son's belongings. Instead of treating them as untouchably sacred (a common and natural impulse) he asked the school to name the boy who would make best use of them. They named Arthur. Whereupon he was invited to make journeys to the schoolfellow's home, in order to carry away these most valuable treasures. I remember his arriving one evening with a large box, on which he had chalked HIGH EXPLOSIVES. 'I had plenty of room in the Tube, mother,' he dryly remarked on his return.

Well, now the shed became all glorious with rows of

bottles, test-tubes, and appliances of fantastic shape. Since Arthur was anxious to keep anyone from tampering with his chemicals, he applied to his more literary brothers for help.

'I want,' said he, 'to put something over the door that will frighten people away.'

'We'll soon find something,' was the reply, and presently there appeared in bold letters this inscription:

ΜΗΔΕΙΣ ΑΓΕΩΜΕΤΡΗΤΟΣ ΕΙΣΙΤΩ

I had to explain this so often to inquirers that I amused myself with ringing the changes on: 'It just means: DANGER. KEEP OFF'; 'It's a Rosicrucian mystic symbol!' 'It's purely platonic, of course'; 'It's only some joke of the boys.'

As far as our immediate neighbours were concerned, we were not warmly welcomed on the Ridgeway. Mrs. Semi-detached did not trouble to disguise her annoyance at our sharing with her the social superiority that she had so lately acquired. Mrs. Lay Reader grumbled at our having turned into a garden her own particular blackberry patch, and the Colonel's wife was distressed because the building operations had driven away a moorhen from the ground. I was duly informed by someone that the Colonel and his wife were extremely exclusive. 'Thank goodness!' was my reply; 'then they will exclude me.' Apparently the curiosity of his wife was stronger than her exclusiveness, for one day I suddenly came upon her round a corner of the half-built house. She was taken aback and full of apologies at her intrusion on my premises. 'It is to Mr. K. you must apologize,' said I; 'the house is not mine yet, because I don't pay the last instalment until the roof is on.' Then we both laughed.

It was by such trivialities that we became acquainted with the other dwellers along the Ridgeway. One would borrow a bit of parsley. Another kept hens and was quite glad to sell the eggs to us. A knock at the door and then, 'Have you got a history of England that we could look at?' The landowner's wife called to ask whether Vivian would give her son some lessons in Latin. It was interesting to see how much more fruitful of pleasant feeling are such exchanges of need than the old-fashioned paying of calls. Even the Colonel, whose dignity was enhanced by his being the only owner of a car, was kind enough to bring me a fine collection of his choicest wallflower plants.

Another thing struck me at this time—how much more productive of good feeling, strange as it seems, a petition may be than a gift. I shall never forget our dismay on the morning of our arrival, when hungry and exhausted we stopped our labours to have some food. I had a tin of soup (and, yes, a tin-opener) and plates, but no spoon. Nor had I the least idea as to which of our packing-cases the spoons would be found in. So I ran across the piece of open ground between us and our late semi-detached neighbour, and stated our trouble. She was already settled in her new house and was able and delighted to lend us some spoons. This appeal to her seemed to wipe out all her jealousy at our having come up from below. I have no doubt that the reason for this may be psychologically unpleasant, but whatever its origin, good feeling is good feeling.

One day I came home to find Barnholt sitting with an

absurdly small kitten on his knee. It had been given him as a gesture of friendship by a dweller on the Ridgeway, who assured him that it came from a very clever stock. So we called it Mycroft Holmes, since he was a shade cleverer than Sherlock. Arthur used to take it round the garden in his pocket, its little head peeping out at everything in a most cunning way. Lerry endured it—no more. He and Mycroft would eat with one another at mealtimes, and made a kind of non-aggression pact. But one thing Lerry found hard to bear. As Mycroft lounged on my lap by the fire, he would lean over and carefully lick Lerry's head. All that Lerry dared to do was to raise his lip one side and show his dog-tooth—but the gesture spoke volumes. When Mycroft was a bit older he would be away for days, rabbiting in our adjoining gorse-grown field, to return tired, muddy, and grossly fat—not hungry, but wanting a drink.

As there was nothing in the shape of a circulating library in the place, our books were frequently in demand. A special favourite with one neighbour was Aumonier's *Ups and Downs*. Again and again she had borrowed it. But one day it was not to be had.

'Sorry,' said I, 'but it is out on loan.'

'How tiresome! I have a visitor who would like to read it.'

'Then why don't you *buy* a copy?' said I, knowing that she could very well afford it. In really indignant tones she replied,

'Certainly not. I am not a collector!'

I kept my tongue as it were with a bridle from saying, 'I see, you only collect other people's.'

71

One visitor we had, a schoolfellow, who had an ungodly habit of browsing among our books and occasionally pocketing one. He brought them back (all, I think, in time), but it was maddening to put forth one's hand for a book and find it missing.

Even the local lady on the Ridgeway was glad to borrow a book sometimes; but she was well ahead of us in another branch of civilization. I was having tea with her one afternoon, when a sound of 'ping-ping-ping' caused her to get up and go into the hall.

'It's all right,' said she on her return; 'we have a kind of local telephone service, and one person is distinguished from another by the number of "pings". My number is four, but I often get confused in counting.'

'How muddling!' said I. 'You must often get odd scraps of other people's conversations.'

'Indeed I do, sometimes rather embarrassing. This time it was only Mrs. Blake ordering a pound of sausages from the shop.'

'The shop' was a development of the tiny business of our early days. It had now become the Cuffley Stores, and harboured a primitive Post Office. And what the postmistress didn't know about everybody's concerns would go on a threepenny bit. As for the provisions, I felt disinclined for them after seeing the cat licking the cheese quite thoroughly.

Soon I had a neighbour in the strictest sense of the word. Mr. K. used the remaining part of our plot to build a house for himself. As it was on the select Ridgeway he could not openly display that he was a builder, for anything in the shape of trade was taboo. So he quite cunningly made a beautifully tiled garage, far too long for a car, and another pretty sort of capacious summer-house across the garden. In these he stored his goods and worked his will on plans and estimates and elevations, and Barnholt remarked one evening, when a light was showing in the summer-house: 'That's Mr. K., bowing down to wood and stone.'

He and his wife have proved splendid neighbours, always near, and yet extremely seldom in each other's house. For my own part, I so dreaded 'callers' in the old-fashioned sense that I never went into a neighbour's house except for some definite reason or request. In this way I escaped an excessive talker, who needed what O. W. Holmes suggested—an inclined plane to bring her to the door; also another neighbour who knew several people with the same little malady that I or one of my sons was suffering, and all with dire results. It used to amuse us to imagine what our neighbours thought we were doing in our secluded nook—invisible from the road. Perhaps a gambling den? Perhaps coining?

However, those who saw the house liked it, and Mr. K. was soon busy enough on new ones, and as he never built two alike, his work became well known for its surprising variety. I believe that when someone wanted a house, Mr. K. used to go into retreat to consider the character of his client before starting on the plans.

Before long Mr. K. had a rival. A speculative builder put up a number of small houses with astonishing speed, and sold them on easy terms almost at once. Mr. K. was horrified at the slenderness of the foundations, and muttered ominously: 'These fellows can put up as shoddy work as they like, because they go away. They haven't got to *live* with it, as I have.'

Houses are like governments—people get what they deserve. Do they look for good foundations, solid structure, staying-power? No; they are fascinated by pretty tiles in a bathroom, or a convenient cupboard. Someone called on me during this period, admired our house very much, and asked me if there was one in the place that she could buy. 'There are some just being built,' said I, 'but I doubt whether the foundations are very reliable—repairs might be needed in a few years.'

'Oh, that doesn't matter,' said she, 'one generally moves to another in three years.'

This attitude to one's house seemed unfortunately to be fairly common, and in due course other speculative builders appeared, had their little day, and then went off to pastures new. Along the Ridgeway, however, several substantial houses were appearing, but the new-comers didn't enter much into Cuffley life. Passing one of these and seeing work in the raw garden going on, I gave some friendly salute and asked how they liked Cuffley. In the tart tones of 'No rags or bottles' came this response,

'We have no religion or politics.'

'All swept and garnished?' said I, and then feared that the allusion might give offence. I needn't have worried, for the answer was,

'No, we are nothing like straight yet.'

A definite push towards the development of Cuffley was the opening of railway passenger traffic to Hertford. We

had more trains, including earlier and better ones. That is
to say, we had one or two expresses. This only meant that
they didn't stop at quite every station. The advantage was
not so much the gaining of time as the lessening of door-
banging. But we had to be careful about falling asleep
coming home, lest we should be carried beyond Cuffley.
Every train stopped at Cuffley, but one evening I was so
fast asleep after a long day's inspection work that I reached
Bayford before I woke, and wondered where on earth I was.

We had to be more careful, too, about catching the train
in the morning. There was a more businesslike tone; none
of the old kindly 'hurry up there please', with a door open
and the porter ready to shove you in. Trains started to
time. We had our own special technique about them.
Vivian and I liked to be ahead of schedule, and usually had
some time for quiet contemplation of the station. Not so
Barnholt, who always left it till the last moment and sprinted
down the hill, with unhappier results than he cared to talk
about. The ideal of Arthur was to walk down at his usual
pace and reach the platform as the train was coming in.
He lived at home longer than the others, and I never knew
him miss a train. Sometimes we would be travelling up
together, and he would send me on ahead (to do my fuss-
ing!). Having given him up for lost, I would hold the
door open anxiously to find him stepping in as the whistle
blew.

That walk to the station, a good half-mile, was the only
thing in our new quarters that compared unfavourably
with the old house. My shopping excursions to Enfield
became burdensome, involving that big pull up the hill

with heavy loads of meat, fruit, and vegetables. But relief was at hand. One of our new neighbours told me that an enterprising butcher in Enfield would call for orders and bring the goods. 'And,' she added, 'he doesn't send more than you order.' And lo, it was so.

Another new-comer told me that one of the London 'Stores' came round once or twice a week, and would bring anything you wanted. The men who stand and deliver have changed as the years have passed, but those Stores still supply all one's dry goods, from biscuits to bedsteads. I said to the deliverer one day,

'You seem to provide everything for our bodily wants. What about our souls? Anything in that line?'

'Well, lady,' said he in obvious seriousness, 'we *have* got a Mission in connexion with the Stores.'

I needed no baker, for now that I had a decent kitchen I was able to bake my own bread again. To complete my independence of Enfield, I was told by Mrs. K. of a farm at Northaw where the people came from Devon, and made butter in the true West-country way. This we have never failed to enjoy as often as it could be brought or fetched.

And laundry? Enfield came to the rescue here, punctually collecting and delivering. All I had to do was to shout to any boys who were at home 'Bring out your dead', make a parcel of it, and leave it outside the door. In due course it returned, all spick and span in blue tissue paper, little black studs and pins. Why, thought I, have a washing-day?

Our little 'kitchen garden' was not all we had fancied. Cabbages never took heart; cauliflowers, when their over-coats were removed, were almost invisible. Red currants and peas did well, but were entirely stripped by blackbirds as soon as ripe; carrots and onions suffered from arrested development. So I was glad to hear from a neighbour that once a week a large rambling cart (from Goff's Oak, I think) brought every kind of ordinary vegetable. And as I had found potatoes heavy to carry, and cabbages bulky, I was greatly relieved to get this service.

Such bits of useful information were usually imparted to me by friends meeting me on the road. Cuffley was so sparsely populated that it was seldom that we met a stranger. Formal calls were quite absurd—they seem to have been killed by the war. However, now and again someone would look in to see how we were getting on.

Among such droppers-in was the Colonel's wife. Spying our piano she casually sat down and played Chopin's Black Key Study. Next morning I walked along the few yards to her house, and knocked at the door. When she opened it, I said,

'I want you to play me that thing of Chopin's again.'

'What!' she exclaimed in genuine horror. 'Play the piano in the morning! I couldn't possibly!'

I was about to withdraw, somewhat abashed, feeling convinced that my informant had been right in describing her as exclusive and stand-offish. So her next words amazed me:

'How do you make your living?' said she. 'What do you *do*?'

My reply was immediate: 'I shook him well from side to side. . . . How is it you live, I cried, And what is it you do?'

'Exactly,' she laughed delightedly, and I proceeded to tell her what I did.

VIII

What I Did

THERE seems to be a widespread idea that writing a book makes one immediately rich. Charles Lamb would have written a funny essay on this popular fallacy, and Pont could make a funny picture to illustrate another of his popular misconceptions. But there is little real fun in it to the author. I had written seven or eight books without any increase to my banking account that would catch the eye. By the time one has subtracted the money spent in books of reference, in railway journeys to collect material, in tips, in meals abroad, in giving copies to friends who think they are 'on tap', and so on, there is actual loss. The wealth achieved is entirely mental. This was notably the case in a book I was asked to write on the City churches. The publisher had been offered a series of drawings of these churches; the artist had only added a few dry notes of facts and dates; so I was asked to make them interesting.

The happy hours I spent slipping about the lanes and alleys of the City cannot be measured in gold. What stores of oddities I found both in people and places; what entrancing beauty I saw in those spires of Wren's against blue skies and rolling white clouds; what friendliness I found, and what deep-set religion, in these old churches—oases of peace in the very heart of the business-centre of the world. I am such a Londoner that I feel more at home in Threadneedle Street than anywhere else—close to the Stock Exchange and Merchant Taylors' Hall.

While I was doing this an invitation came for me to meet an American author, distinguished for her successful guidebooks on various countries. She received me hospitably in a sumptuous apartment of one of those big hotels in Park Lane. She was attended by two secretaries, and like Dogberry had everything magnificent about her. In the midst of bright conversation and delicious sandwiches she said,

'You are engaged in writing about the City churches, I hear. Now do tell me *how* you set about the job—how you gather your facts.'

'I go in and sit down in a pew,' said I, 'and let the church talk to me itself.'

'Oh . . . oh,' said she, in a puzzled manner. 'Is that all?'—and soon dexterously changed the conversation. I felt from her manner that I had turned out to be disappointingly dull, and had no heart to tell her how often from my pew I had noticed in the dim light a hard-boiled City man coming in to kneel for a few minutes in prayer. In fact all that I had seen appeared trivial and absurd in that fine hotel.

This author had plenty of gay anecdotes to tell me of her experiences in London, but for real inside information there is nothing to equal the ordinary City man. Such a one lived near me at Cuffley, and asked me (when I told him what I was doing) whether I knew of a restaurant in the City where they said grace every day at one o'clock before dinner.

'Some ancient religious fraternity?' said I.

'A pretty ancient fraternity,' said he, 'but not religious.

It is (originally) a Billingsgate fraternity, and it is a fish dinner, and business men of all kinds come in, hang up their hats and sit down to table as if they were at home. An old fellow of ninety, who comes up from Brighton every day for this duty, puts on an apron, says grace at the stroke of one, and then ladles out the soup for all. And there are other odd ceremonies. You ought to attend it.'

'Can a woman come?' I asked.

'Oh, yes, I'll take you any day.' And he did. And I have often been there since, and a friend of mine had her wedding breakfast at this midday lunch.

Among my odd ways of eking out a bread-winning capacity was a specially pleasing one. On several occasions I was asked to give a summer course of lectures to men and women of varying ages from country districts, assembled in a conveniently central town. The subject was Scripture, and I was allowed a free hand as to syllabus and treatment. The audience consisted mainly of teachers from all types of schools, with a sprinkling of young clergymen. I encouraged questions and remarks as the work went along, and in this way often obtained a 'modern' explanation from a student, when such a statement put forth by myself would have shocked. Nevertheless there was always plenty to be said that was bound to shock. I had long come to the conclusion that unless you shock people you make little impression. And it was obvious that they enjoyed being shocked, for it broke some restricting band, and let them breathe more freely and taste reality. Sometimes I detected a happy little laugh from some older member of the audience.

Curiously enough it was the young students who were

most inclined to entrench themselves in received opinions. A determined young woman once waved her flag bravely; sitting in the front row she glared at me in a most discouraging way, and at last one morning burst out, 'I think the Catechism is quite enough. I have taught all the children in my class to know the Catechism, and they have all passed well.' 'If,' said I, 'you feel the Catechism is enough, don't waste any more time with me. I can't imagine why you are here; don't mind going out at once.' But she refused to budge.

Another teacher approached me one day after a lecture with a large limply-bound Bible open in her left hand; placing her right hand reverently over it she said, 'I refuse to regard the Bible as literature.' I tried to point out that vast portions of the Bible are in poetry, that our Lord used poetry, striking little stories and witty epigrams, to clothe his truths—but she was adamant. I fancy that 'Literature' in her school had been a water-tight compartment. Her attitude was on a par with that of a headmistress I know who forbade her staff to bring any 'outside' history into Scripture lessons.

The clergymen obviously enjoyed my excursions from the ordinary. 'I agree with all you say,' said one to me in the intimacy of our evening discussions, 'but I daren't say them myself.' Another vicar, a fellow lecturer, said one evening over a late cup of coffee, 'It seems to me that you choose from the Gospels just those things that you think Jesus was likely to have said and done—from your idea of him as a whole—and you neglect the things that conflict with it.' 'Tell me,' said I, 'as man to man, don't you do exactly the same? Unconsciously? Hardly aware that you are choosing? Aren't there some words attributed to Jesus that you never take as a text for a sermon?' I suggested a few examples. 'Yes,' he admitted; 'you are right; we do choose what we feel is in harmony with the whole character.'

No, it was not from the clergy that I met with opposition, but from young fundamentalists. One group of malcontents thought it wise to lodge a protest with the bishop of their diocese, detailing my lax views and bad influence. Later on the kind secretary of the lecture-course sent me the letter that the bishop wrote in reply. It was to the effect that he had made full inquiries as to what had been taught, found that Mrs. Hughes had only expressed his own views, and desired his thanks to be conveyed to her. My reaction to this was a desire to frame his letter and hang it in the hall as a kind of testimonial, just as my brother had felt inclined to frame an apology he had received from his bank.

There was one type of objector with whom I felt specially sympathetic. 'I cannot bear,' she (it was usually a woman) would say to me privately, 'to give up any belief that was taught me by my mother.' My reply always took some such form as this: Imagine yourself a mother, teaching your children the best you possibly can. Would you like to think that when you died they were always to be bound by what you said, even in the face of wider thought and sincere conviction?

It was in such intimate conversations with students and cheerful talks with fellow lecturers that the most easily recalled part of these summer courses lay. One such conversation I remember with special pleasure. I chanced one morning to sit next to Walter de la Mare at breakfast. He was conducting a course of English literature, and I had seized an opportunity to attend one of his lectures. We began discussing Keats, and I ventured to suggest that perhaps his early death had been in a way fortunate—that he had done his best work.

'No, no,' was the emphatic reply. 'No, he would have got over the Fanny Brawne episode, and *then*——!'

'What glorious stuff you gave us yesterday about him!' said I. 'But why do you *read* your lecture?'

'I don't understand,' said he. 'What else can one do?'

'You are full of matter about Keats; you could talk for hours about him, now couldn't you? Why not discard your notes, and let yourself go?'

'Face that audience without my notes? Why, my knees would knock together!'

'Let them knock, Belshazzar, no one will notice it behind the desk. Then your eyes will be free to watch your audience—then you can see whether they are following easily or looking puzzled—perhaps go more slowly.'

'Did I go too fast for them?'

'You did indeed!' I laughed, and added: 'You know the story of Wesley's first extempore sermon? He lost his manuscript on his way to church, and confided his despair to the old caretaker. "Can't you trust God for a sermon?" said she. He plunged, and never used notes again. That gives me an idea: look here, when is your next lecture?'

'Soon after breakfast—9.30 this very morning.'

'Give me your notes. I am returning to London this morning, and I will post them back to you.'

'Ah, no, I couldn't be without them at hand. But I'll really have a shot at what you say.'

To cheer up our last cup of tea, I asked him if he had heard the story of the Scotsman who paid the taxi-driver sixpence too much. Of course he hadn't, and riposted with another story of similar tone, about two moths flying out of a Scotsman's purse, and we parted in laughter.

It chanced during one of these lecture courses that an important inspector descended upon us. His impending arrival was announced at the breakfast table, and caused some consternation. He won't inspect the Scripture, thought I, and if he does I don't mind; I know too much about inspection to dread an inspector. So I went about my work unconcerned. But I was mistaken about his avoidance of Scripture. We were in full swing when he entered upon us. I offered him a chair near me, and he sat down, note-book in hand, as for a continued seance.

'We are studying the Exilic Period,' I explained, 'and the blending of the various ancient legends in narrative form. At the moment we are taking as an illustration the story of Cain and Abel, and inquiring into the historical facts underlying the statement that Cain's offering was rejected. Now would you help our discussion by giving us your opinion on this subject?'

'The fact is,' said he, rising, 'that I have to go on to hear some other work. . . . I'm afraid I cannot stay.' He went out, and we went on.

This incident confirmed the opinion I had already formed that an inspector should never vie with a teacher in knowledge of the subject in hand. His business is quite otherwise, and confession of ignorance in some abstruse point is no disadvantage to him. In fact it may be a positive advantage. If this man had said, 'I have no idea why Cain's offer was refused, but I am interested to hear your explanation. Please go on with your discussion'—he would have soon discovered all an inspector needs to know. In fact I have found it useful in my own inspections to pretend ignorance, and ask a teacher a question she is sure to know, in order to get over her nervousness. A fellow inspector told me that on one occasion a history teacher, with whom he found some fault, rounded on him with the question, 'Are you, may I ask, a history specialist?' 'No,' replied my friend, 'I am not. I am a specialist in inspection.'

Teachers naturally dislike being inspected, but the inspectors sometimes have unhappy moments too. I have often wished during the many years of this work that some other name could be devised for them. 'Inspection' is strictly correct, no doubt, but it suggests prying and fault-finding, whereas its real purpose is encouragement and sympathetic advice. I have found that no one minds being set right on some points after other points have been praised. Only twice in twenty years' work can I recall teachers so bad that I could find no single point of merit. The severest criticism (did they but know it) is not to find fault, but to omit to invite them to a private talk. The written report has its obvious uses, but it is in those private and informal chats between inspector and inspected that the best work is done.

Sometimes such a chat consists entirely of naming a man's good points, for if he has been trying fresh experiments he is glad to hear an outside view of them. For instance, a history teacher had contrived to avoid the necessity of any boring revision lessons. He compared any newly mentioned statesman or soldier or policy with something similar already studied, but in each case got the comparison from a member of the class. He feared that this used up too much time; but I assured him that history was usually taught far too fast—with too much detail, covering too much ground, and cumbered with written notes. He, however, was keeping the great events and personalities and policies always within the pupils' grasp, as it were. I made him laugh by describing a woman teacher I had heard who had excellent qualities but ruined her work by insisting on 'covering the syllabus'.

Such an interview was entirely pleasant for both of us, and makes a curious companion picture to another. Above all things I enjoy attending a good Latin lesson, and walked into a middle form one day in lively expectation. The master was a young Cambridge man with high qualifications, but gave a lesson that showed no single redeeming feature. I felt that he would be sensitive to adverse criticism, and I would fain have slid quietly away. But the headmaster asked me to have a few words with this master in the library.

I walked to the library in no cheerful mood, with no idea as to what I could possibly say—perhaps the best preparation for a difficult interview. As I took my seat I heard myself saying,

'Your lesson this morning made me very unhappy.'

To my amazement he replied, 'Not half so unhappy as it made me.'

'Anyhow,' I exclaimed, 'we are agreed on one point, and can begin. How about your other classes?'

'Oh, I get on well enough with the beginners, and also with the upper forms. It's these tough IVA that beat me.'

I laughed. 'Of course that's always the case. Ask the rest of the staff. Beginners in any subject are enthusiastic, and advanced classes are tasting the joys of scholarship. It is in the middle that unusual teaching power is required. Now you and I together ought to be able to manage something. You have a far wider knowledge of the classics than I have; and in the course of many years of visiting schools I have picked up all sorts of teaching ways; let us pool our resources.'

He soon agreed with me that both the beginning classes and the advanced classes got their pleasure from a sense of *new power*—from being able to say a few words in Latin, to being able to appreciate a Latin poet. What sense of new power can be produced in IVA?

'They get so bored with translation and putting English sentences into Latin,' said he.

'Of course they are. Who wouldn't be? Both are grossly overdone. And the essence of boredom is knowing what is going to be done.'

'But you can't avoid translation,' said he.

'A great deal of it you can. "Caesar in Galliam contendit" surely doesn't need it. If you read aloud slowly and well, and get the class to do it too, they often get the sense with some little help as to new words. The more "impossible" things you expect of people the less bored they are. Even Caesar can be made attractive. And if you are not tied to a set book, find some short and easy bits of Latin that are enjoyable. Can you suggest some?'

'Oh rather,' said he, and began to suggest a few of Martial's amusing epigrams, some lovely lines of Catullus, some famous bits from the *Aeneid* and the *Georgics*, a letter of Pliny's. . . .

'Stop,' I cried in delight. 'You've got the idea.'

'Yes, but how about putting English into Latin? Can that ever be palatable?'

'Let them feel their power—not in managing "snags", but in turning any bit of English into Latin. Open a history book out of a desk and try to put a sentence from it into Latin. Don't be too fussy about the grammar at first—they can find their own real howlers.'

'Yes, grammar. How can that be kept warm and improved without a lot of grinding?'

'It can't. There must be grinding. But concentrate the grinding into short bits. It's a good plan to have two or three minutes at the beginning of a lesson spent in parsing round rapidly the first lines of a piece of Latin. This keeps the accidence warm and trains them to notice the endings. Then for syntax you can let just *one* point arise out of the reading. Don't feel you have to explain every difficulty that turns up immediately it turns up. But let them feel that every time they have achieved something worth while.'

'I can't get copies of books for them. Would you write the new thing on the blackboard?'

'A better plan is to dictate it slowly, and as you walk round you can set right any mistakes—the dictation is not a test, but a mere convenience.'

'Our school secretary would help now and again by typing a few copies for me.'

'That would be fine, and the copies can be kept.'

Last of all I told him of a lesson to a middle form that I had recently heard, where the headmaster showed the construction of a Latin sentence by reading it aloud in different tones—loud and firm for the principal clause, subdued for the subordinate clause, and still softer for a sub-subordinate one. This amused the class, and they enjoyed trying this feat for themselves. By the time two or three had read it, the meaning of the whole rolled out.

That was many years ago and I expect I shall never see this young man again, and I have no faintest recollection of his name or of the name of the school, but that dreaded interview remains one of my pleasantest memories.

Oddly enough it is often conscience that does the worst damage in teaching. It is particularly rampant among women teachers, and especially young ones (for older ones have learnt better). Not only do they insist on 'covering the syllabus', but also on setting long written exercises, and correcting every slip in spelling and punctuation, passing over weightier matters of English style or historical fact.

After pointing this out once to a young teacher, I hazarded the guess that she probably spent hours every evening over her neat, red-ink corrections in these (indicating one of several piles of some thirty note-books, assembled for my inspection).

'Indeed I do,' said she, in a gratified tone of conscious rectitude.

'Then I fear you are not very conscientious,' said I.

This was such a shock to her moral system that she could only gasp, 'Not conscientious!'

'A much bigger duty than correcting spellings is to come before your class fresh-minded and good-tempered—with some little historical surprise or new way of seeing old facts. Now, listen, your history is good, and needs little more than looking up. Make a point of going a walk, or having an evening with a friend who doesn't teach, or go to a film—any bit of change, and see whether new ideas come to you, of far more value to your class than your red-ink corrections, which I know on good authority that they seldom read.'

On the other hand, I came upon a young man taking a large class of small boys in history. While he was walking about among them, aiding and abetting them over some map they were constructing, I picked up a few note-books, and found a great deal of native spelling unreproved.

'What do you do about spelling faults?' I asked him when we were alone, and added, 'I'm only asking out of curiosity.'

'Nothing,' said he. 'I've as much as I can do to get some sensible notions of history into them. If I niggle them too much over spelling, I shall lose touch. Of course I take care to put up on the board any proper name, such as Caractacus, and come down hard if it's misspelt.'

'I heartily agree with you,' said I, 'for your history work with that class is too good to be altered in any way. I may suggest, however, that any boy who is a particularly bad case in the spelling line might be mentioned to the English specialist—there are ways of dealing with this trouble, and bad hand-writing, too—without encroaching on the short time allowed for history.'

A case of enlarged conscience, or perhaps misplaced endeavour, appeared in a school in Northumberland. A class of small boys were reading aloud a short poem of Wordsworth's, in the broad accent of their county. The teacher apologized to me afterwards for their style of speech, and said how assiduously she was endeavouring to correct it.

'Correct it?' I exclaimed. 'Why, I was thinking as I listened to your class, how gladly Wordsworth would spare an hour of heaven if he could hear those boys speaking his poem as it ought to be. Don't correct them, whatever you do.'

But she obviously thought me peculiar, and void of the refinement she had hoped to see in an inspector from London.

At the other end of the country, in the sixth form of a large London Roman Catholic school, a learned lesson was being given on Chaucer. The master muttered half to himself, 'This, to have its full effect, ought to be spoken in Lancashire dialect.' 'Do read us a stanza in that way, Father,' said I. And forthwith he did, to the obvious delight of the class and myself.

These inspections helped greatly to keep the pot boiling, of course, but they also kept me mentally 'on the boil'. Apart from the pleasure of hearing good lessons in a great variety of schools, I enjoyed the talks with my fellow inspectors in the hotel after the day's work. Each of us was a specialist in something, and eager to pick up views from one another. Especially was this the case when I worked for the Board of Education. In the evenings, round the fire or in a corner of the coffee-room, we discarded talk of the school, and chatted of this and that. One man knew all about Einstein's theory, and for a brief hour made me think that *I* did. Another man's dream was to spread a universal language (Ido or Esperanto, I forget which), and he made me think for a short time that it was a Good Thing, although in my bones I hate the idea.

The most lovable of my fellow inspectors, Dr. Davison, had made a lifelong study of earthquakes, and when he mentioned the word, I burst in proudly with,

'I myself have been in an earthquake; it was in the nineties, when I was staying with a friend in Camden Town—the bed rocked under me.'

'Ah yes, that was on May 9th, 1896,' was his immediate rejoinder. 'You see,' he added, observing my astonishment, 'I have written a book on earthquakes in England.'

'A whole book on English ones!' I exclaimed. 'And others on earthquakes all over the world?'

'Yes, a nice little row of volumes,' said he ; and added with a wry smile, 'the worst is, nobody will buy them.'

'But then, think of your fame as an authority,' said I.

'Yes, indeed, I am famous, but my fame consists entirely in being the father of a champion motor-cyclist.'

Another fellow inspector was a brilliant talker on almost any subject that turned up, but he had an Achilles heel. I was drawn aside privily by the others on our arrival, and told, 'Whatever you do, don't let So-and-so get on to the subject of anti-vivisection; it's a regular King Charles's Head with him.' It may have been anti-vaccination, which I always confuse with anti-vivisection, but I know it was anti-something, and I enjoyed watching the skill with which these conversational pilots avoided any possible approach to it.

It was customary to devote one long evening to minute discussion of the school in all its aspects—buildings, programme of work, head, and staff. Comparing notes, we saw more than one side to a teacher, sometimes corroborating our own view and sometimes modifying it. We were quite outspoken, making no choice of epithets, as we should be obliged to do in our written reports. Those informal consultations were a real safeguard that each teacher would be treated fairly.

On the last day we had a final meeting with the governors of the school. We all attended, so as to answer any questions, but the main business was the talk of the chief inspector. It was an intellectual pleasure to see how fully and succinctly he described the general impression given by the inspection as a whole. I remember one such occasion when we had been doing a large Church girls' school. The governors were all present, and among them some rather important Church dignitaries. This is how the chief inspector ended his remarks:

'You will conclude from what I have said that we have warmly approved every aspect of the school life that we have observed, and can highly commend the principal and staff, the discipline and all the material surroundings in this beautiful neighbourhood. It is a free country, and it is no part of the duty of the Board of Education to suggest aims to any school or to impose a curriculum.'

After a pause he added, in a careless, smiling undertone,

'But I myself, speaking as a private individual, would never send a daughter of mine to a school where science is not taught.'

I shall never forget the faces of those clerical governors—the sudden drop from pleasant satisfaction to discomfort, and on the most important of them a look as of the 'Soul's Awakening'. I am quite sure that science was introduced into that school, and that the personal touch had done far more than any argument.

One job fell to my lot that will rouse pity in anyone who has had to undertake a similar one. It was not remunerative, and if I had only been quicker with a cast-iron excuse I might have escaped it. A school that I had inspected asked me to give away the prizes. As it was to be weeks ahead, no excuse was at all plausible, and I am one of those weak people who will promise anything if it is a good way in the future. They might forget. I might die. Measles might break out. But of course convenient things like that never happen. A reminding note reached me.

In a light-hearted way I had several times advised some miserable friend what to say on such an occasion; but my suggestions had been turned down as too unconventional. In fact there seems to be a definite 'frame of reference' at these functions. It is easy enough for royalty or the very great, for they need only smile and wave the volumes. Inferior people have to make a speech under three main heads: general remarks on education, manners, and morals; warm praise for the distinguished scholars; consolation for those who have won no prizes. The very thought of it induces a yawn. I felt that my only hope was to preserve the framework, but say exactly the opposite of what was expected.

While the venerable chairman was doing his preamble, the headmistress whispered to me, 'We hope you will speak for at least twenty minutes.' I suppose there is no audience more nerve-racking than a hall-full of schoolgirls, when you are on a platform, with all your deficiencies of manner and attire in full view.

I began by describing modern youth as most people regarded it—lacking in common courtesy, indulging in slang, regardless of the aged, especially aunts, and so on. These sins were not peculiar to our post-war time, for a letter had been found, written two thousand years before Christ, in which an Egyptian says to his wife, 'My dear, I don't know what the young people are coming to.' Then I gave my own view of modern youth—that it was better than the enforced courtesy of Victorian days, more thoughtful of others, more open. Then I instanced cases I had noticed in that particular school, and in my own sons (some of these made them laugh).

The people who had gained distinctions and prizes were deservedly happy enough, I said, but I had a word of encouragement for those who had not shone. 'As I was coming down here in the train to-day,' I said, 'I happened to be reading about a woman who had never shone in school but had married a distinguished man of science. "I was the ideal wife for him," she says, "for I cooked him excellent meals, I mended his things, kept his books and papers tidy, looked after his accounts, and—this above all— listened to him." There you are, girls, think of the future you may have if you marry a learned man, and take heart.'

Another chance of adding a little to the family coffer came my way at uncertain intervals: I was asked to address various women's institutes in remote country places. A small fee was accorded, and my fare, and (a great boon) the subject of the talk. I looked upon these as sheer jaunts, for the main trouble of any talk is the picking of the subject. They were so pleasant, as to the places I saw and the people I met, that they have faded into a rosy background. All save one. In one I lost my temper and my manners, and also my self-respect, for it seemed like obtaining money under false pretences. But it is delightful in retrospect, and so has stuck in my memory.

The prescribed subject sent me was 'Luxury and Waste'. An odd and unpleasant mixture, thought I, for a talk to village women. In short, it smelt to heaven. But there was no choice, and I prepared some elastic notes.

On arriving at the country station, I was taken by car to a finely-appointed house, amid lawns and trees and conservatories, and then received by two courteous maiden ladies. An elegant lunch was served and followed by a much-needed cup of coffee. For during the meal my hostesses had done nothing but impress on me the kind of *line* they wished me to take in my discourse, without a word of inquiry as to what I had prepared.

'Surely,' said I, 'you yourselves have had ample chances to impress your views on these women—why an outsider to do it?'

'Well, you see,' said one lady, 'it would seem rather personal from us. They are so improvident in spending their money on pink silk blouses and high-heeled shoes, and so wasteful in throwing away bones that would make a nourishing soup—little points that they would suspect we had noticed—but a strange lecturer would have a wider and more impersonal touch.'

'Quite,' said I, and thought of the very nourishing soup that I had just enjoyed, and could have informed them of the cost of it, in addition to the 'old bone' foundation.

'And another thing,' said the second lady, 'these women are so hard to influence, because they keep themselves *to* themselves. At any of the meetings when we have tried to start a discussion, it has been impossible to get them to say a word.'

'I will try this afternoon to get them to say a word,' said I.

'You won't succeed, we can assure you,' was the pitying reply.

As I was swept along in their resplendent car to the meeting I felt vaguely annoyed, and when I saw my audience I was angry. In that sordid village hall, unrelieved by anything beautiful to look at, and windows too dirty to look out of, sat rows of patient women prepared with gloomy resignation for forty minutes' boredom. Casting my notes aside, I burst out on these lines (adding any lively anecdote that came to mind whether to the point or not): 'My subject is Luxury and Waste. Now as to Waste, I am sure that none of you waste anything you can possibly use, either in food or clothing; and you don't want to listen to a lecture on cooking and sewing. So let us give our thoughts this afternoon to Luxury. For myself, I believe in luxury. It is a grand thing. What exactly is luxury? When we have done our work and our duty and all that, luxury is that little bit of extra pleasure that we enjoy. We could do without it, of course, but it sweetens life.'

Then I gave a lot of examples—a bright-coloured blouse, a gay hat, a bus-ride, chocolates, and so forth—and watched the faces in front of me relaxing a bit. And I was glad to realize that my hostesses were on the platform, well behind me.

'Of course,' I went on, 'we have to remember that what one person thinks a luxury, another might dislike. It is amusing to think that a king and a beggar are alike in this—neither can have exactly what he wants. Here is a little story I came across that will show this: The king of the peacocks was strutting along his lawn, showing his breast of royal blue, and the flashing colours of his train. In the gravel at the end of the lawn some little sparrows were fluttering in the dust, and the royal peacock turned to watch them. But the attendant guards ordered them away. As the day went on various amusements were brought to his majesty, and in the evening his chief attendant asked if there were anything else he could possibly desire. "I would like above all things," said the king, "to have a good roll in the dust." '

Then I grew fierce, and said that there were two things to warn them about, of the utmost importance. The first was that luxury must always mean real enjoyment. High-heeled shoes must not be bought merely because Mrs. Bloggs has them. A new hat may be bought to please one's husband, but not to outshine Mrs. Griggs. My second warning was

that our luxuries must not mean depriving others of theirs
. . . or frowning on them as wasteful. 'Your husband,'
said I, 'must not only be allowed, but really induced to
enjoy his baccy and his beer, his games, and his friends.
And your children must be allowed their luxuries, even
when these clash with your ideas of tidiness in the home.
Very funny some of these luxuries are. For instance, my
youngest boy at one time got immense pleasure from going
round the room without touching the floor. An odd idea
of luxury, but there it was. It involved threading his way
along the window-sill, navigating the mantelpiece, and
walking over the piano.'

'Oh! *Not* the *piano*!' exclaimed one of the women.

Hurrah, the village had spoken. Soon we were in a
lively discussion on the bringing-up of children. My time
was gone all too soon. Not caring to catch the eyes of my
hostesses, I slipped through the door, and taking a leaf
from Sisera's book, fled away on my feet to the station.

It was recollections of this kind that I told the Colonel's
wife when she asked me what I did. Instinct told me that
she had not asked out of mere inquisitiveness, nor (still
worse) out of a merely polite interest, but out of genuine
sympathy with a widow's struggles. She became therefore
my one exception among the Cuffley neighbours to the rule
my mother taught me. She had culled it from Lord Chesterfield, and it ran something like this: Be really reserved with
everybody, and seemingly reserved with nobody; for it's
disagreeable to *seem* reserved, and dangerous *not* to be.

IX

Outside Events

As little as possible about my sons' lives will come into this narrative, but a few bare facts are needed for clearness. It had been the hope of my husband and myself that they should all go to the university. By this he meant Oxford or Cambridge, for he was quite definite that in the matter of universities it was: Oxford and Cambridge, and the rest nowhere. My own appreciation of the value of the life at these places was based on three things: a man is in touch with the best brains in his own subject; he meets men with all sorts of ambitions in the way of careers; and, best of all, he makes lots of friends.

As for the value of a degree—I am not so sure about that. One amusing incident in Barnholt's career was the fact that he got a job merely because he said in his letter of application, 'I have an Oxford Honours degree, but hope this will not stand in my way.' Believe me, this was for a post on a newspaper.

When a chance came to him for work in Tanganyika, he was ready enough for the adventure, but it was one that I would gladly blot from my memory. It was grand experience of life, but brought him within an ace of death. He had two attacks of black fever, and was ordered home, and forbidden ever to return. A week spent in Capetown with our old friends the Bournes helped to pull up his health. On the journey home he sang out lustily one day his imitation of an old porter at Finsbury Park: "Arringay, 'Ornsey, Woodgreen, New Southgate, Oakleigh Park, New Barnet, 'Adley Wood and Potter's Bar—Potter's Bar train.' His steward came running up. 'Oh, sir, do *you* know that old fellow? Why, I *live* in Wood Green!'

We all went to meet Barnholt at Waterloo. He looked glad to see us. In our taxi-drive to King's Cross, he kept leaning out to gaze with delight at the familiar landmarks of his beloved London. 'There it is, not altered a bit!' was his constant exclamation.

In spite of all the new building, traffic regulations, and neon lights, London never seems to change its heart. To-day, as ever, like Dr. Johnson, we can 'take a walk down Fleet Street' and capture the same spirit. But while Barnholt was away there had been an astonishing thing happening in London. One Saturday afternoon an Oxford friend of Barnholt's was having tea with Arthur and me at the *Thistle* in the Haymarket when we heard cries of 'Paper! Paper! Starnewsstandard! Paper!' more vociferous than usual. Looking down into the street we saw on the placards, 'General Strike Monday'.

England acts like a fruit-tree with a branch injured. The whole tree pours its sap (or whatever it is) into the branch so that it bears more fruit than the other branches. It was a never-to-be-forgotten effort that the country made to live through that strike. The first thought was to bring milk for the children, and ample supplies were brought by private cars and stored in Hyde Park. Trains, managed by unskilled hands, were few, very jerky, and far between. But private cars! The roads were long processions of them.

Papers had to be produced by volunteers, and were treasured as priceless by those who managed to get them. I have kept several as curiosities. Our Sunday *Observer* was typewritten.

The strikers tried to interfere with bus-drivers, and I remember one bus that had a notice written up: 'The driver of this bus is a Guy's Hospital student. The conductor is a Guy's student. Anyone who throws a brick will soon be a Guy's patient.' For bricks were freely thrown by the strikers at anyone and anything. One notice ran, 'Keep your bricks. All windows broken.' And one bus so afflicted announced itself as 'The Aerated Bus Company'.

The few cars that Cuffley possessed were used to take our business men to town. Its coal supply was not enough to take a train up our incline to Crew's Hill. So our station was closed. And as there was some suspicion that our stationmaster had 'red' leanings, a watch had to be kept on the station. For this purpose Arthur was chosen. Merchant Taylors' School had an enforced holiday, so he embraced the job whole-heartedly. Each morning I saw him off (with sandwiches and so on), dressed in his cadet uniform, and carrying concealed in a deep pocket a policeman's truncheon. One day the stationmaster came to ask if he might go into the booking-office. 'Certainly not,' was the reply. 'But I only want to fetch my umbrella,' pleaded the man, upon which Arthur unlocked the door and gave him his umbrella. I rather gathered that Arthur enjoyed much time in the signal-box, exploring its mysteries.

I thought myself fortunate to have no work away from home, except an examiners' meeting in the south of London, which would of course be postponed. But I had an urgent message that I must come at all costs, and the costs would be theirs. So off I started 'brave and early', and by means of hitch-hiking, with a few train and tram rides thrown in, contrived to be in time for the meeting. One experience is vivid in my memory. For some absurd reason I found myself walking down Edgware Road. Seeing a young man in a two-seater, I held up my hand. 'Where to?' said he as he drew up. 'As near to Victoria Station as you happen to be going,' said I. Often have I been down Park Lane, but never in such a royal way as that. At Victoria I managed to get a train of sorts, but no food had I achieved. How glad I was of the good tea served round to the examiners, and to hear the experiences that each had endured. One of them gave me a lift on the return journey, and I got a train that crawled as far as Winchmore Hill, to find myself one of a crowd of dwellers farther north, eyeing the road for a lift in a private car. It seemed ages before I saw a Cuffleyite with room for one, but it came at last, and I reached home very tired and hungry. And yet somehow exhilarated at having seen the faces of Londoners, usually set and serious, suddenly become by misfortune full of gaiety and *bonhomie*. A revolution, I thought, will never succeed in England— the victims will be giving lifts to their executioners.

A week of it was enough. Arthur received a 'handsome letter' from the Prime Minister, thanking him for his national service, and all was soon forgotten and normal again. One change it made in Cuffley, however. The very few of us who had a wireless set invited their neighbours in to listen to the news. Of these Mrs. K. was one, and how startled I was to hear the voice of the announcer speaking as clearly (and apparently as nearly) as if he were in her room. And even now, accustomed as I am to all kinds of broadcasts, never can I get over the mystery of it—made far more mysterious when the thing is portable, and independent of any means of support or connexion.

Another addition to the amenities of Cuffley at this time was the gramophone. I had been distressed by early specimens of this invention, and hoped never to hear another record. But of course, as in the case of the wireless, a really good gramophone was a revelation. When we had one of our own I scented a curious drawback to it. I have never mentioned it to people, because it sounds silly, but I wonder whether anyone else feels the same. I am fond, say, of a certain piece of music, and its performance by a master is a moving experience. With a gramophone I can have it for the mere putting on. My dread is that I may do this once too often, and thus deprive myself of that experience. I keep off it, as a drunkard would keep off the bottle. A visitor dropping in is welcome to put on whatever he likes and no harm done; it is one's own personal control of the thing that seems to me disastrous, when one lives alone.

Yet another modern convenience reached Cuffley at this time. An old typewriter was passed on to me by a friend, and I fancy it was the first one to reach the neighbourhood. It was a Yost, large and loaded with strange devices, but Arthur very quickly taught me how to use it. Where he had learnt himself I never inquired. It came in most opportunely, because the publishers of the Latin book had asked me to concoct a book about England for foreigners—just to give them some idea of what we were like as a nation. It was intended to be a kind of guide as to how to behave in a restaurant, how to buy a pair of shoes, and such banalities. I agreed to do it, of course, but I had no sooner started than the whole thing ran away with me. Anyone with his head screwed on can point to a pair of shoes, or an item on a menu; he can go to the Tower, the Abbey, Madame Tussaud's, and all the other sights, under good direction. But I wanted a foreigner to know something of an Englishman's love of the sea, and of the horse and of grumbling; to be able to see the beauties of an out-of-the-way village, an old inn, a Roman road; to know which newspaper to rely on, which to be amused with; to comprehend, if possible, what an Englishman thinks funny. I got several contributions from my neighbours in Cuffley, and I wrote to Vivian at Oxford, asking him to do me a whole chapter on our railways. To my delight his chapter was a description of a journey in a *slow* train—an item in a guide-book that I have not elsewhere come across. It was typical of the whole book, which conveyed the idea, 'Take your time in England if you want to see it as it is.'

The publisher demurred, but said he would risk it, and it turned out a success and still sells after fifteen years. Barnholt said it was badly written, pointing out usefully where and how, and I could but agree with him. On the whole the family was a bit ashamed of me.

Barnholt had not been long at home when he said that we ought to be on the telephone. Both he and Vivian were trying for posts, and they knew that being on the phone would make them readily accessible when anyone was wanted in an emergency. It saved the bother of a letter and the delay of waiting for a reply, and gave one a chance, Barnholt added, of impressing an employer by one's manner and readiness. Several of our neighbours had held out against this innovation, feeling sure that their wives would be using it recklessly, or be always calling them up at the office. So we were among the earliest in Cuffley to have it installed. Arthur and I were alone when we were rung up for the first time. How we both made a mad rush to the lobby, falling over one another in our eagerness not to keep our friend waiting! As the boys predicted, it has been a great help in endless ways of business matters, and to be without it now would seem like losing one of the senses. The countless messages I have received have cancelled one another in my memory—all but three which can never be forgotten. But these came a little later.

It was not uncommon for me to be rung up to meet some little local emergency, with talk like this:

'Can you come to our Conservative meeting at 3 this afternoon? We are short of speakers.'

'What's the subject?'

'For and against Socialism.'

'Right. I'll come. Oh, by the way, which side do you want me to take?'

'For. There are plenty of people against it.'

'Right. I'll come.'

Sometimes it was not the phone that caught me. Once I fell a victim in the little Post Office. There I was on my lawful occasions when a Ridgeway neighbour spied me, and began, 'Could you possibly help us? We are in such a hole! The speaker for our Mothers' Meeting hasn't turned up, and the next train won't be in for an hour. Will you give them a short address?'

'On what subject?'

'Oh, anything you like,' was the callous reply.

'But do give me some idea.'

'Well, we would be glad if you could bring in the Church somehow.'

This was a degree worse than her other remark, and while the local President was opening with prayer, I tried to collect my wits. They are all women, thought I, and mothers, with long odds that their children are lively and apt to find Sunday the dullest day of the week, and possibly to connect religion with this dullness. Why not face the fact? So I started with a paraphrase of this reflection, and found it shocking enough to gain the attention of the lumpiest mother. Then I told them how I had had three lively boys of my own, and was anxious for them to have some happy associations with Sunday and religion (beyond, I added hastily, the pleasures of Church attendance). As Sunday is usually a day of what you must *not* do, I devised some things that were only allowed on Sunday. I spun this out a bit, by describing the boys' Sunday Box—full of all sorts of tiny toys, collected gradually from crackers and Christmas bazaars, such things as usually get thrown away —some even saved from my own childhood. Then each boy had his own Sunday Book; a home-made collection of sheets of paper, with hand-made illuminated cover. In this each would paste a picture of some Bible subject, look up the reference, and write a text underneath. Of course it takes a little time to collect things, but friends help, and the children must do all the *doing* themselves. The great point is that no single thing must be done except on a Sunday. With this stuff, and answering questions, I managed to stay the course for a quarter of an hour.

Soon after the excitement of our telephone installation, we had the chance of an ancient excitement in the heavens. A total eclipse of the sun. The two elder boys were away at work, and Arthur was to join a scientific expedition from Merchant Taylors'. And I, left alone, felt an urge to see this 'once in a lifetime' exhibition. Looking at the newspaper map which showed the area of totality, I saw that Portmadoc was in it. So I wrote to my old friend there, whose house stood on one of the lovely hills of the town, to ask her if she could put me up for one night. Of course she could. It was a bit of a squeeze, for I was not the only one with this request. We had a jolly evening, and went to bed early so as to be up in good time for the show.

Wales came out strong. 'I'll give you eclipse,' she seemed to say. It was pouring. We all put on macintoshes and walked out to the top of the slope beyond the garden, to find scores of the townsfolk already in position. With our eyes glued to the spot where the sun ought to be, we kept exchanging views on weather probabilities. But the thick cloud persisted, nor did the rain slacken. Watches were consulted and the exact time of the totality was upon us. The only effect I noticed was a slightly deeper shade of grey in the sky, and a slightly chillier chill. And even these may well have been mere imagination. We could but laugh, all of us, and hurry back to a hot breakfast. The servants, of course, had been out too, and I had the curiosity to slip into the kitchen and say to the old cook,

'And what did you think of the eclipse, Martha?'

'Oh, indeed, it was terrible! The sun came flashing through the sky in a flame of fire—like this!' And she dashed the carving-knife through the air with a mighty swoop. Obviously the word 'eclipse' had indeed literally fired her imagination. This scrap of conversation gave me food for thought about reports on miracles.

Welshmen will not be surprised to hear that the following day was gloriously sunny, and beautiful Portmadoc looking its best. I had arranged to travel back on a through express with a restaurant car. So I begged my kind hostess not to give me the sandwiches that she was plotting.

'Ah, but you never know—at a time like this,' was her reply, as she insisted on preparing a basket for me.

How wise she was became evident before long. That train turned out to be neither through, nor express, nor provided with a restaurant car. It looked as if all England had turned out to see the eclipse, and was endeavouring to get home. Our train had a corridor indeed, but it was too full to be a useful passage. We stopped continually, probably for the engine-driver to find out which was the least congested route to take. This provided me with one of my most delightful memories: we were taken through the vale of Llangollen. It was my first sight of that bit of paradise. How pleased we all were that the train had to stop there, and then go on slowly. It was worth all the eclipses in the sky.

Then came another unexpected delight. No refreshment

of any kind was to be procured from the railway company; and many passengers had relied on it. Consequently there was widespread hunger towards midday. Then came the real miracle—like a small edition of the Feeding of the Five Thousand. Everyone with a basket of provisions offered to share its contents with all within reach. And amid great laughter everyone had plenty of sandwiches, fruit, lemonade, buns, and chocolate.

And now for one of my three ever-memorable calls on the phone:

'Speaking from Cambridge. Can I have word with Mr. Arthur Hughes?'

'Sorry, he is not at home. Will you leave a message?'

'Kindly tell him that he has been elected to a major scholarship at Trinity Hall.'

I needed this bit of cheer. When my husband died I figured to myself that I had strength for ten years' work, and if I could launch the three boys into independence by that time I should feel satisfied. But as it turned out things were not so simple. Vivian had not been able to do more than just keep himself. Barnholt was at home after his illness in Africa, anxious to take any work that offered, so as to relieve the privy purse, as he called the home maintenance. Teaching he loathed. What he wanted was work on a newspaper, and there's nothing like knowing exactly what you want. Weary weeks went by in answering advertisements and visiting the offices of local papers, with no result. A friend gave him an introduction to an influential man in the Press world, and a meeting was arranged in a London hotel. After preliminary chat, this kindly man said,

'What you want, my dear sir, is a job on the *Telegraph* or the *Morning Post.*'

'Yes,' said Barnholt hopefully, 'any kind of introduction——'

But this piece of information was *all* the man had to say.

Determined to earn some money, Barnholt then took some temporary teaching jobs, each one providing him with secret amusement or fresh scenes. One took him to Budapest. Another was coaching the son of a wealthy family; at lunch one day there was rapturous talk of the beauties of Switzerland, and presently a lady turned to Barnholt with 'Have *you* ever seen a snow-clad mountain, Mr. Hughes?' 'Only Kilimanjaro,' was Barnholt's reply.

To invigilate at a school examination was easy work, but to take the place of an absentee master in a preparatory school was another business. It was only for a week or two, and Barnholt agreed to do it—with a wry face.

'Look here, mother,' said he, 'I've got to take English and Latin—that's all right, but History and Scripture! Suppose some little wretch asks me when the battle of Tenchbrai was fought, or who Eli was—I'm done for.'

'Quite simple,' said I, 'if you are careful to tell them *nothing* that they ask. You must watch your step, or you will slip out the future of *rego* to some lazy inquirer. Make them look up everything; give them lessons on the use of an index, a map, a dictionary, an encyclopedia. If you never tell, they will never find out your ignorance.'

On his return he thanked me fervently: 'Mother, that tip of yours about knowing nothing was just a talisman.' He had had no trouble with the discipline, for he knew little boys' tricks. He described how one day he was sitting at his desk doing corrections, while the class were doing preparation. With the tail of his eye he was aware that a boy was gradually and stealthily edging towards the end of the form he was sitting on, with the glad hope that it would tilt up with a terrific crash. It did. But Barnholt never lifted his eyes from his desk, and the boy had to put the form back with no drama.

'Yes, mother,' added Barnholt, when I laughed over this, 'it's easy enough to outwit the boys, but after all it's only a subtle way of bullying—the master is always top-dog by his sheer intelligence, and it seems a shame to take advantage of it.'

I gathered that he had had some very pleasant hours with those little boys, and that the best teachers are often those who don't like teaching. A widely experienced trainer of teachers asked me casually one day, 'Does teaching, do you think, by its very nature make people unpleasant, or is it merely that unpleasant people are drawn to the work?'

Soon after this last experience, Barnholt gained what he wanted, a foothold in the office of a newspaper. Here, it was not his ignorance but his knowledge that had to be suppressed, for the editor, like the customer, is always right. At the week-ends he used to come home with funny instances of this. Here is one I remember: the editor had decorated his opinions with some sort of metaphor involving the words *virgo intacto*. Barnholt, eyeing the proof, said, 'That word should be *intacta*, shouldn't it, sir?' 'Ah, no,' was the reply, 'you see it is Latin, and has to agree, *virg*o *intact*o.' When I asked how he had reacted to this, Barnholt shrugged his shoulders with the remark, 'What does it matter what he says in his footling leaders!'

But he was learning a great deal about the working of a paper, and never grumbled at any disagreeable task (of which there were not a few). He made me think of an anecdote Mrs. Bryant once told me in my schooldays: a boy applied for a job, and was asked what he could do. 'Anything, sir,' was his ready answer, 'that you give me to do I shall do better than anyone else.'

I used to look forward to the week-ends when he came home, for we had grand talks on politics, religion, and the future of Europe, as well as such things as the seamy side of advertising. It was a new idea to me that the Press is not absolutely free.

X

Comings and Goings

THE Welsh terrier, Lerry, and Mycroft, that mighty hunter, had been members of the family for so long, that it was quite a grief to Barnholt on his return from Africa to be told that Lerry had died of a ripe old age, and that Mycroft had stalked one rabbit too many. We never knew what became of him, and if we heard a loud mew outside we would run to the door, hoping to see him stagger in. His successor was a beautiful kitten named Feste, full of promise for housework against the mice and as a decorative feature about the place. But she kept bad company: a neighbour's cat used to entice her to go out after the rabbits, and one morning the tempter arrived home with a piece of wire round his neck—alone.

We were not left long without a cat. The owner of the woods had a remarkable one; it had been found, when quite a kitten, tied up in a basket and left by the road, mewing piteously—evidently abandoned by some dastardly motorist. It grew up to show itself a semi-Persian, with astonishing hunting-power, and, moreover, an instinct to bring home her kill, instead of gorging abroad as Mycroft had done. I was promised a kitten, if she should be blessed with offspring. One day I was invited to come and make my choice from a litter of five. They all looked alike, but when I noticed one of them struggling to get out of the box, and succeeding, I said, 'Give me that one.'

'What shall we call it, boys?' said I when I had brought it home and unveiled it. Barnholt, who at the moment was full of a book of Eddington's, exclaimed,

'Call it the Second Law of Thermo-dynamics.'

This soon became shortened to Thermo, and when any visitor showed curiosity as to its origin, I had two explanations ready: if the inquirer was a man, I told the truth; if it was a woman, I said it meant 'hot stuff'.

Indeed she turned out to be hot stuff in keeping the rabbits within bounds. Not content with their fine gorse-grown field, with lots of excellent cover, these pests have always preferred to get through our hedge and eat our lettuces and young greens of every kind. I have taken a dislike to eating rabbit, or enjoying their pretty tricks. They seem to me no more than vermin. I remember asking my mother once,

'Did God make black-beetles, mother?'

'Certainly not, darling, they are vermin,' was the immediate response. I can also remember the next question that rose in my untutored mind, but I had put it aside as irreverent.

In dealing with rabbits Thermo had the true military instinct; avoiding the traps of the open fields, that had caught Mycroft and Feste, she captured the enemy appearing in the garden, and also discovered their base—the mound over the roots of our big oak, where they reared their families. Here Thermo would sit like an image, waiting her chance to pounce. Often I would reward her by skinning her catch, and giving it to her in decent portions. I never petted her, and perhaps for this reason we were great friends. She would dash about the garden with me, running up and down trees just to show off. Often when I returned from a day's work to an empty house, it was most welcoming to hear through the door, as I put in the key, loud purring. It seemed like sheer welcome, for she was quite able to get in and out of the house by a window at any hour, day or night.

Her affection for Arthur gave him two real 'turns'. If late out at night he was accustomed to come in quietly so as not to disturb the house, and go upstairs in the dark. It was a shock on one occasion to stumble over the corpse of a rabbit, headless and blood-stained, laid as an offering at his bedroom door. The other experience was worse, because uncanny. A corpse after all is a corpse, and can do no harm: it is life that frightens. He was putting the key in the door one dark night, when he felt his hat being gently tilted from his head. Thermo was poised over the porch, stretching out a welcoming paw.

Thermo would often go with me to the station, leaping along by the hedge. But it was a dangerous adventure, and her love of darting away from cars only just in time eventually proved fatal. Going out to post a letter one day I found her lying dead, obviously run over. The kindly motorist had laid her gently on the grass, and I was able to give her decent burial. How badly I missed her company.

A four-year-old boy in the village had begged one of her kittens and I had given him one, named Mr. Pooter (although sex was uncertain). When Thermo died, I sent a message to him that I must be sure to have any kitten that Mr. Pooter produced (hoping for another Thermo). In due course Mr. Pooter grew to be a magnificent semi-Persian tom. Again in due course a kitten appeared in the vicinity, the living image of Mr. Pooter, and was duly sent up to me. It was the little boy's urgent request to the person who brought the kitten that amused all: 'Be sure,' said he, 'not to tell Mrs. Hughes that Mr. Pooter didn't have the kitten him*self*. She would be so disappointed if she knew that it was the black cat at the farm, who really *had* it.'

My dislike of cars had been steadily growing. I had endured being taken for rides by a patronizing neighbour (involving gratitude and admiration); a car had abandoned Thermo's mother to its fate; a car had stolen, presumably, a valuable pedigree pup that had been given us after Lerry's death; a car had killed Thermo in the prime of her life. But how different was my view of a car when once I handled the controls. It came about in this way:

A friend of Barnholt's in East Africa, named Moran, came to visit us. We owed Barnholt's life to him, no less; he had managed to get Barnholt into a hospital when he was at death's door with malaria, and had taken care of him like a brother. But it was not only gratitude that won our affection for him. He was an enormous man, a great traveller, a fascinating raconteur, and at home in any circumstances. Barnholt said that short stories were always happening to him. Indeed, he could turn the slightest incident, by his gestures and tones, into something thrilling. For instance, he once kept me in a dreadful suspense while he described how he had taken a girl into a country café, and ordered tea in a lordly manner. To his dismay he could feel only a sixpence and some coppers in his pockets. He himself 'never ate with tea', but the girl did. Desperate measures were crowding his mind when the waiter brought the bill. 'Yes, yes,' said I, impatient for the denouement, 'how much was it?' 'Sevenpence half-penny.'

In quite another vein Moran's practical ability was amazing. Barnholt told us how he would get an engine working when it seemed beyond repair, and missing 'essential' parts. This kind of situation was not uncommon in East Africa, where the natives thought that if an engine wouldn't go, the god *in* the machine was angry and they had better decamp; or else they tried to beat it into good behaviour.

Now Moran had a car, an *n*th-hand Austin Seven, which he brought to show us, and take us anywhere we wanted. I looked out one day to see Arthur in it, careering along the garden path and going aground in a bed. But Moran was quite unconcerned. 'He'll soon learn,' said he, 'if he's left alone.' Shortly after this one of Arthur's schoolfellows came to see us, and Arthur offered to take him to the station, without mentioning that it would be his first essay in navigating the road. The schoolfellow caught his train, and after seeing him off Arthur saw a distracted woman carrying a baby, hurrying up just too late.

'Where were you going?' asked Arthur.

'To Enfield, and there won't be another train for an hour.'

'I have a car here,' said Arthur; 'allow me the pleasure of driving you to Enfield.'

And this he managed, without giving the woman any

grounds for suspecting what a strange adventure she and her baby had been in.

I have often pondered on the oddity that the best teachers are those outside the profession. Moran's masterly inactivity with Arthur accomplished far more than a lot of instructions and warnings and hints. His method with me was of the same kind. He put me in the driving seat, sat beside me to inspire confidence, made me quite clear as to the difference between the accelerator and the brake, and then said: 'I want to go to Cheshunt this morning. Drive me there.'

'Oh, I couldn't possibly,' I insisted.

'You've got to. And you can if you've got to.' And I did.

But Arthur had to descend to his bicycle again, for he was going up to Trinity Hall. When he had settled down a bit, Moran took Barnholt and me to see him. The Austin Seven jibbed a little at the hill up to Goff's Oak, but Moran got out, appeared to be speaking firmly but quietly under the bonnet, and the hill was climbed. Fortunately most of the road to Cambridge is flat, and we got there in time for the lunch Arthur had prepared for us in his rooms; it finished with the best cup of coffee I have ever tasted. 'How did you make this?' I asked. 'Your old recipe, mother: put in as much coffee as will do, double it, and pour boiling water on it.'

There were two visits that I had to pay in Cambridge. One was to introduce Arthur to my husband's tailor, a friend of long standing.

'You have two other sons, have you not, Mrs. Hughes?' said Mr. Neal.

'Yes, but they both went to Oxford.'

'Oh...oh...Oxford,' said he, in a tone of deep commiseration, as though I had told him of their untimely death.

My other visit was to my oldest friend, Mary Wood, then head of the Cambridge Training College. The boys shot me in at the front door, promising to call for me later, knowing how much two old school-fellows have to say entirely between themselves.

It was not old schooldays that Mary and I talked about, unless it was to laugh at our old school song. This was *Forty Years On*—an adaptation of the Harrow song to the needs of girls. One line of it referred to our condition forty years on as being 'weary and broken and seeking God's rest'. We felt like Falstaff, not come to that yet, even after more than forty years on.

Our talk lay mainly in discussion of present difficulties. Mary's troubles were mostly with her staff.

'What is it so peculiar in a staff that makes for trouble?' I asked. 'They are all devoted to you, I'm sure.'

'Oh yes, quite. It is a sort of internecine warfare that seems to breed in a staff-room.'

'The other day,' I said, 'I was praising a lesson, just attended, to the headmistress, when she commented sadly, "Ah, yes, her history is excellent, but in the staff-room she is a perfect scourge." '

'And it's so difficult to get rid of them. Students come and go, but one's staff is more like the brook.'

'Are you trying anything new with the students?'

'Nothing new, but I'm trying my best to avoid their being too much absorbed in their work when they start in a school—to get them to cultivate some outside interest, even if it's only a hobby.'

'I'm heartily with you there,' said I. 'Young people respect a teacher who has some interest beyond attending to their mistakes, who is *good* at something.'

'Yes, and it might blow fresh air into the staff-rooms even!'

'There is something infectious about an absorbing interest. I've come across a curious instance lately. One of my fellow inspectors was telling us of an odd thing he found in an elementary school. The master of the eldest class (of course boys under fourteen), when asked what they were doing in arithmetic, said, "The differential calculus." '

'How absurd!' said Mary. 'He must have been joking.'

'Exactly what the inspector thought, and said as much. "Well then, come and see them," said the master, and led the way to his classroom. There, sure enough, were the boys hard at this work, and so intent on it that they barely looked up at the stranger coming in. "You see that little fellow over there in the corner," said the master, *sotto voce*, "he is one of the best; but he always works with one leg tucked under him, as you see him now. I tried to break him of the trick, but his work immediately went to pieces—so now I let him do it." '

'I'm glad of that,' said Mary, 'but what I want to know about this master is why he first started such a venture.'

'That is just what the inspector wanted to know; and the master was quite candid about it. He had been bored, he said, with the dull problems in the text-book, and of course the boys had scented his boredom and caught it, and did as little work as possible. So he took them into his confidence one day, confessed his own boredom and his own passion for mathematics, and asked them if they would like to taste its joys. That was all.'

'How jolly!' said Mary. 'But what did the headmaster say to it?'

'He was a gem, and encouraged originality in any form.'

The boys arrived to collect me all too soon, but we all had a final cup of coffee over Mary's fire.

New Cambridge friends of Arthur's were soon on our Cuffley threshold, in addition to the schoolfellows of Merchant Taylor days. The name of one schoolfellow visitor was impressed on my memory—Jordan—because there was a smack of the irreverent in the telegram announcing that he had passed some examination. Barnholt at last discovered a means of distinguishing Arthur's friends from those of the rest of the family—they never sat on chairs: couch-end, floor, tables, piano—yes, but not chairs.

A large number of the boys' friends brought the girls of their choice to see me, and as time went on their wives and nowadays their little ones—all greatly to my delight. But when one of the earliest schoolfellows brought a second wife, close on the death of the first, I found it difficult to be decently polite. In fact, I don't think I succeeded. He had been so desperately stricken with grief over the death of the first, seeking sympathy, that it seemed hardly decent to arrive so soon with a gay young substitute. He is the only friend we can be said to have lost. Others will crop up at any moment. For instance, I returned from work one evening expecting the lonely hearth, to find Moran happily installed over a bright fire. 'Blessed woman,' said he, 'to hide the key in the same old spot, so that a fellow can get in after being away seven years in India.' By the way, I shouldn't be surprised to see his head round the door as I write these words.

And now for an event in my own private life. Early in 1928 I had a letter from Middlesbrough to say that my brother Tom was ill, and could I possibly manage to come to see him? I am old enough to know what that kind of message implies . . . one may be too late. Years before I had had an unhappy experience in this way. Hearing that my old aunt Tony in Cornwall was very ill and clearly not likely to live, I hesitated whether to go to see her, or to spend the journey expenses on comforts that I knew she might well be unable to afford. I ended by sending a cheque to my cousin in charge, explaining my mental debate. What a fool I was! I am certain now that when one is dying no material comfort has the slightest value in comparison with the sight of a beloved face. That is the blessed viaticum for one's last journey. To add to my bitterness, the stupid cheque was returned to me with the news of Tony's death, and the statement that the money had not been required, and with no word to let me know whether she had been even told of it.

Tom should not miss me, if I could possibly manage it, and I started off at once. It was a long journey, giving time to think. Tom had been a widower for many years, and in 1927 had married a golf-companion. This had pleased me greatly, and I was looking forward to knowing her, for he made the strange admission that he was having the happiest time of his life. (By the way, how little one knows of apparently smooth home lives!)

Reaching the house in the dark, after a tram-ride to a suburb of Middlesbrough, and much groping to find the right number on the door, and dreading to ask how Tom was, I was greeted by a bright face and the words: 'He's expecting you.'

How the old boy beamed with pleasure as I came up to his bed! He knew he was dying, but had no worries about the hereafter. Nor the need. Just as he had done throughout his life, he was spreading jollity around him. As far as his strength allowed he told me some funny stories that he had been saving up for me, including the riddle, 'Which is the greatest invention of the century?' The shadow of death surely never fell more softly and affectionately. He used to say that he had kissed my head when I first appeared in the world, and now it seemed fitting that I should kiss his head as he was leaving it.

XI

Another Venture

ONE morning a solemn family council was held. We had come, as Vivian expressed it in episcopal style, to a veritable parting of the ways. No, the family was not about to break up; for indeed the chief force of its cohesion has always been its continual going and coming. The first article on the agenda was, 'Shall we buy a car?'

I had invited a guest from South Africa, Hilda, the only child of our old friend Bourne. She had not been to England since the days when she had visited us years before, and played with the boys in the mud-pie period. She had accepted the invitation, and was now actually on the ocean.

The argument *for* a car was put strenuously by Barnholt. The guest must be shown something of England. He could drive, and the worst English roads were child's play after the best of African ones. Vivian was *against* a car, as being a wild extravagance, when trains were always to be had. Arthur was at Cambridge, so the casting vote fell to me. I don't know who the Frenchman was who said that he could do without life's necessaries if he could have its luxuries, but I have always felt it a sound dictum. 'I'm *for*,' said I; 'and now for ways and means.'

The second article on our agenda was the need of a garage. We felt sure that Mr. K. would build us one somewhere along our little drive. I reckoned that I had enough money to pay for the garage and buy a small car. Vivian obviously felt like the small boy who refused to learn the alphabet, because you never knew where this sort of thing would end. But Barnholt set off for London.

Walking into one of those spacious shops, where a few disdainful cars unveil their beauty to passers-by, Barnholt was greeted by a nice young man.

'Were you thinking of a car, sir?' said he, waving his hand airily towards a Rolls Royce.

But Barnholt was not to be impressed by an Oxford manner, and answered, 'Yes, and what I have in mind is an Austin Seven.'

Preserving his courteous manner, the young man then led Barnholt through miles of serried cars to a more congested department, where jolly little Austins looked all eager for the fray. In due course one was selected, tried out on the road, paid for and delivered. I shall never forget seeing Barnholt drive it in. Both of us were reminded of the incident in *Rudder Grange* when they manage to buy their very own horse and trap.

'Come along, mother, get in, and I'll drive you to Enfield.'

Meanwhile Hilda was plugging along the ocean. Her boat was due at Tilbury at 3 o'clock one afternoon when Barnholt started in good time to fetch her. Vivian was away from home at this time, or I think he would have smiled rather triumphantly at Barnholt's difficulty. Tilbury by train from St. Pancras—easy as falling off a log—but Tilbury from Cuffley by car was beset with endless snags, and Hilda was ashore and beginning to wonder what to do next, when at last Barnholt arrived and packed her happily into the little Austin.

On the roundabout route to Cuffley Hilda suddenly burst out with 'Oh, stop! Oh, look!'

'What's the matter?' said Barnholt.

'Why, there's the *Bell*! And you said we were in Edmonton.'

'Well, what of it?'

'But that's where John Gilpin didn't dine!'

'Oh, if you are going to stop at everything literary or historical in England, we shall never get home.'

Indeed the whole country seemed to Hilda packed with delights, natural and historical. Her excursions had to be limited, because the boys were all at work, and could snatch only week-ends for drives. In those days there was no such thing as a driving-test before you got a licence. You just paid your five shillings and had the freedom of the road. Hilda soon learnt to drive by herself, and asked me airily one morning if there was anything I wanted—she was agog for an errand.

'You might get me a book of stamps at the Post Office,' said I, for by this time our 'all-in' shop had a grill at one side and dispensed stamps, postal orders, old-age pensions, and all.

'Right,' said Hilda in a business-like tone. 'Back in a few minutes.'

More than a few minutes went by without any sign of her. I concluded that she was having a chat with Mrs. Martin, the postmistress, an inevitable accompaniment to buying stamps. But I was getting a little anxious when at last she returned, a bit shaken. She had got down to the Post Office safely, a *facilis descensus*; but it was turning round on the up-hill that was the *opus*.

'What does one do, boys,' said I, at our next family gathering, 'when the car won't go, and you are somewhere on a country road?'

'Get out, sit by the side, and look pathetic,' was the succinct advice.

It was obviously an iron code in those early days of car-driving never to pass an apparent distress without a shout of 'Can I help?'

When there is a car in the family it is often difficult to know at any given moment where the members of the family may be. It chanced one Sunday evening that I was quite alone. Hilda was away staying with relations, Vivian was away at work, Barnholt had gone to Cambridge to see Arthur, and might return any minute. It was dark, and I was reading by the fire. I had not bothered to draw the curtains after enjoying the sunset. A tap on the window surprised me, and I looked out to see a disreputable sort of man. Supposing that he was in need of food, I called out, 'Go round to the door.' Now in the care-free style of Cuffley life, I used to leave the door unlocked, but at this moment some instinct made me dash round quickly and turn the key in it. I had only just done this when the man, instead of knocking, was rattling the handle to walk in. Rather terrified, I went to the telephone and called up my good neighbour, Mr. K. 'There's a man in the garden, trying to get in,' said I in a shaky voice. 'Coming,' was the immediate reply. Very soon there was a loud knock at the front door, a reassuring shout from Mr. K., and there he stood with his kill. He had not waited to come round by the garden gates, but had leapt over the fence and collared the man. Holding him firmly, he managed to call up the farmer who acted as our local constable, and then Potter's Bar police station.

The house was soon the scene of excessive busy-ness. One very tall policeman was taking down notes on my statements, others were testing all the windows, various neighbours had appeared, and Mr. K. was keeping hand and eye on the culprit. More than once Mrs. K. rang up to ask whether her husband was still alive. A phone call from Hoddesdon told me that Barnholt and Arthur were on their way. 'Right,' said I; 'there are sausages for supper, and the house seems full of policemen.' Then I slid into the kitchen and put the sausages to cook.

The inquiries, the note-taking, and the sympathy of the neighbours went on. 'How can you possibly live in this house alone?' 'Fancy not drawing the curtains!' were the main lines of thought. In the midst of all this neighbourly concern, a low voice at my elbow came from one of the under-bobbies, 'I think, mum, your sausages want turning.'

It was only in later years that Mr. K. told me what happened in his leap over the fence: the seat of his Sunday trousers was torn right across, so that it had to be mended by a tailor. No wonder his temper was a bit short when his wife kept phoning to know how he was. He asked me to reply, 'Go and boil your head', or words to that effect.

In due course we had to go to the Court in Hatfield to give evidence, and I had to take the oath for the first, and I hope the last, time. It turned out that the poor fellow was well known to the police, and no doubt his 'three months' were the best thing for him. I have had no repetition of such an incident. 'Nor want', as the fishmonger sympathetically remarked.

After this the boys felt a bit anxious about leaving me alone; but fortunately Arthur soon got his Ph.D., and was allowed to keep a car. This meant that he could spend nearly every week-end at home, and was within reach in an emergency. The Austin Seven began to show signs of weariness, and Arthur set his heart on a Riley. Moran helped him put the Austin into as good form as possible, spent hours washing, polishing, and straightening out bulges, and then set off with Arthur to a second-hand car-mart. A lovely Riley looked too good to be true, a tourer with no defects. Arthur was staggered at the amount allowed him on his Austin, and he and Moran drove off in the Riley as hurriedly as possible lest there should occur some change of mind.

A few days later Arthur was returning in it from Cambridge when he was held up by a policeman at South Mimms.

'What have I done now?' said Arthur, jumping out.

'Nothing wrong, Sir,' was the smiling reply; 'I only want to congratulate you on your car. It was mine until a few days ago, and sorry I was to part with it, for it's a beauty to go. For family reasons I had to sell it—much to my grief. I wanted to tell you how glad I am that it has fallen into the hands of such a capable and courteous driver.'

A companion picture to this occurred in Cambridge. One day Arthur came out of his rooms to see a policeman brooding over the parked Riley. Expecting to be fined for over-parking or some other misdemeanour, Arthur was agreeably surprised to hear, 'I was only just admiring your beautiful car, Sir.'

The boys had trained me never to sit up and get anxious if they were late. Well, I knew it would spoil their pleasure if I did; and they were quite capable of finding something to eat, or making up a bed if they brought home a friend for the night. One night I heard the click of the electric light in the small hours, and was glad to know that Arthur was safe back. In the morning he told me what had happened: he was about half-way home when he came across a dreadful scene. A man and his wife lay dead in the road, police around, a disabled car, and a young Cambridge man standing by looking hopeless. The accident had been entirely the fault of the victims—of that there was no doubt, but of course the young fellow was completely unnerved.

'Where do you live?' asked Arthur.

'Off the main road, away to the east; I was going home.'

'Get in here by me,' said Arthur; 'I'll drive you home.'

The gratitude of the father and mother was rather touching, and I felt rewarded for never having shown anxiety if the boys were late.

One night a Cambridge friend was brought to Cuffley in the Riley. The route is tricky, varying from a broad speedway to country roads, with many villages and side-issues. But Arthur was so accustomed to the run that he kept at a good pace, in spite of some fogginess, rather alarming his friend now and again by his sudden and confident turns. At last, however, a protest was lodged:

'I say, Hughes, do look out; what is this infernal narrow lane you have plunged into now?'

'Oh, it's all right, this is our drive.'

This same friend was a crack car-driver. And one day a phone message from him invited Arthur to come to Scotland and help him in judging some car contests, and begged him to be in Scotland by the following day.

'What a jolly holiday,' said I. 'You'll have to start at once. I'll get lunch ready while you pack your things.'

'Quite, certainly, a very jolly holiday, but I don't budge from this house unless you have a holiday too. That's flat.'

I knew by the set of his face that it was no use arguing. And it seemed such a shame to let a holiday in Scotland go. For myself I knew no friend in Scotland, nor have ever set foot in it. But many a pressing invitation had I had from my sister-in-law Carrie, in Middlesbrough.

'Very well then,' said I; 'if you can drop me in Middlesbrough on your way to Scotland, and pick me up on your return, I'll go.'

'That's grand,' said he. 'How soon can you be ready?'

'I've only got to throw a few things into my case, arrange about the milkman, and so on, and ask Mrs. K. to stop any burglars. In fact I can be ready as soon as you. Just send a wire accepting, and another to Carrie. How soon can we reach Middlesbrough?'

'By to-night easily, if we start at 2.'

'I feel rather loose coming off like this,' said I, as we set out.

'That's just the fun of it,' said Arthur.

At Knebworth there was an ominous rattling behind, but it was only the name-plate come unstuck, and that was soon put right. At Newark we had a puncture, but that was mended while we went to a shop and had tea. Our real trouble began when we tried to find Middlesbrough. It was getting dusk and we had to get out to read the signposts. 'Where's Yarm?' said Arthur, reading one. 'No idea,' said I, 'but I've heard of it, if that's any use.' At last we reached Thirsk, and got clear directions for Middlesbrough. But it was now dark, and although the roads seemed townlike, there were few people about. We asked a woman to direct us to Oxford Road. She was like myself about Yarm—she had *heard* of it, but rather thought it was not in this part of Middlesbrough. 'Part!' I exclaimed. 'Of course Middlesbrough is a big town and has parts. I remember now that the district is called Linthorpe.'

By the time we had found Linthorpe and then Oxford Road, it was 11 o'clock. We began then to grope along for the number, when we spied a beam of light from a front door, and Carrie and her sister standing at the gate. They had supper and a grand welcome for us. Arthur would not spend the night there, but said he must push off for Scotland. He told me afterwards that he spent the night somewhere among the Cheviots, wrapped in a rug in the Riley. He told his friend that he had been delayed owing to giving his mother a lift. 'Ho!' was the reply; 'then that accounts of course for this young lady's hat in your car!' The fact was that I had put my best hat (a rather youthful one) in the back of the car just as we were starting, and forgot to take it out at Middlesbrough.

The next few days were a case of a good time being had by all. While Arthur was enjoying perilous moments in judging the driving in Scotland, Carrie was showing me the glories of the Yorkshire moors by daily excursions in her own car. Scenery is unspeakably glorious to see, but boring to read about. I must mention, however, one small experience that would interest any literary person. A few miles from Thirsk, we came upon the village of Coxwold.

'This is the house,' said Carrie casually, 'where Sterne wrote *Tristram Shandy*.'

'Stop!' I cried, and stared my full. There are few houses one wants to buy at once to live and die in. This was one— small and low, close to the village road, decorated with branching trees against the walls, looking so old that I felt sure they had been lovingly planted by the old scoundrel himself, in the intervals of his writing. He must, too, have written sermons of some kind, for immediately opposite the house is the church where he was curate. I suppose there are few settings of famous books so unspoiled as this village, which looks as if it hadn't turned a hair for nearly two centuries.

I was glad to see Arthur again safe and sound, and we started for home one sunny morning, going by the coast in order to avoid the Doncaster races. Here again one high spot stands out. We had breasted a hill, and spread out in front of us was a wide view that looked like the whole of Yorkshire.

'Stop!' I cried. 'We can't hurry past this.'

'Right,' said Arthur; 'let's get out and have lunch here on this bank.'

Coxwold and all Yorkshire—not bad for memories of one holiday.

After this I was less recalcitrant when Arthur suggested a little holiday somewhere, and on his saying, one fine morning, 'How about lunch in Wales?' I merely gave a gasp of delight and quickly got my case ready.

Yes, we had the lunch I had managed to put together in a field just over the border, and reached Aberllefeni and Corris, our objectives, in the early evening, and by the time we had visited the old home of Fronwen, stood a little by my husband's grave, and visited the few of his friends who were still in the place, we began to think of supper.

'Let's go to the *Slaters' Arms*,' said I. 'How often Dad has told me about it. They will give us a meal of some kind.'

But Corris was not what it used to be. They could raise a cup of tea for us, but nothing beyond a few weary biscuits to eat with it.

'Come on quick,' said I; 'it's Machynlleth for us,' and we dashed along that best of all valleys by the side of the Corris river, to the *Wynnstay Arms*, where we had some food and rooms for the night. The food included a blancmange, to which we still refer with a grin.

'Where next?' said Arthur, as we climbed into the car after breakfast.

'Could we possibly get as far as Exmouth and look in on the Drews?' said I. 'There's a jolly hotel—the *Beacon—*

where I've been staying on an inspection in Exmouth—we could spend the night there, if you can possibly get through to Devon in one day.'

Arthur gave me a scornful look, and let in the clutch.

That drive through the middle of Wales was new to both of us—a kind of path that even the vulture hadn't seen, full of grand Welsh names of villages, which we could pronounce to perfection.

As we drew near Exmouth we became conscious of hunger, and spying a telephone-booth at a cross-roads Arthur said it would be a good idea to let the Drews know we were coming to supper. 'You see,' said he, 'as a member of the A.A. I have a key that will admit me to any telephone-booth,' and he jumped out and applied it. But there was no impression made by it. I forget whether the key failed or the exchange failed, but we deemed it best to hurry on or all chance of supper would melt. In fact, by the time we had booked rooms at the *Beacon* and reached their door, the Drews had reached the coffee stage. But they soon produced a fine supper, and we talked late into the night.

These people had been our near neighbours and best friends in Cuffley, being none other than the exclusive Colonel and his wife. They had left Cuffley in disgust on account of the increase of badly built small houses and general destruction of its 'country' character. They had now acquired a villa in a short cul-de-sac in one of the best parts of Exmouth, with a fine garden, and a tree-fringed field beyond. Yes, they seemed fully justified in having deserted poor little Cuffley. But there is a sequel to this story. Only a year or two had gone by before a vast pink gasometer was built on this delightful field. One gathered, from the not fully expressed feelings of the Colonel, that during the noise of the building operations he could have suggested some points to Dante.

But anyhow we had that jolly evening with our 'neighbours'—a bright spot before returning home next morning. And they were glad to see us, unmistakably, although we must have made a big hole in their larder.

Since we had first known these neighbours they had acquired their only child, a little girl whose upbringing I had taken the utmost interest in from her birth. She was in bed that night when we burst in upon them, but her mother had some of her sayings to tell us. And one I think is worth repeating as a kind of summing up of commercial wisdom. Little Alison lost her bucket, and her mother was commissioned to buy another.

'What kind of bucket shall I get, darling?'

'The goodest one for the lessest money.'

As we drove home the next day I told Arthur how much I missed these people in Cuffley. Some of our present neighbours were of such a different calibre. I instanced the remark of one of them when I said I never minded when the boys came home.

'Oh!' said she. 'How unfeeling! How unmotherly!'

'So just to lead her on I added, "Neither do I ever ask where they have been." This genuinely shocked her—it seemed to spell a lack of proper interest in their welfare.'

'Proper,' laughed Arthur, 'that's the word, mother. It's the proper thing with people like that to show agitation when anyone is out late, and they think their infernal inquisitiveness "motherly". I shall never forget Barnholt's remark to you once: "Do you know why we always tell you where we've been? It's because you never ask." '

Such conversations were always scrappy, because Arthur never took his eye from the road, for 'there's always a fool round the corner'. Indeed I remember two occasions when such a fool dashed round upon us, and we were within an inch or two of an accident. In specially tricky places we used to invent new 'famous last words', such as 'Here we are at Camden Town.' Conversation, though scrappy, was apt to be the more interesting because short-lived—broken off at dramatic points (designedly perhaps) and never renewed. Thus, for instance:

'Getting one's Ph.D. is very pleasant, mother, but it has snags.'

'How so?'

'Well, you know my rooms in Peas Hill. The other night, quite late, a woman from a house across the road came rushing in and calling for a doctor. I was fetched, and said I wasn't one—I had nothing to do with medicine. But the poor woman persisted that I *must* be able to help, and that her daughter was in dire trouble, and not a moment to be lost.'

'Goodness, Arthur, how dreadful! Whatever did you do?'

'I went over and did the best I could—— Look at that fiend, swinging out like that without giving a signal.'

When the traffic was less congested, I renewed our talk, but carefully not at the point of interruption.

'Any other snags?'

'Yes. I was at a dance in Cambridge, soon after Degree Day, sitting out with a girl—don't know her name—and some of our fellows went by, and called out "Hullo, Doc!" As soon as they had passed she turned to me and said, "So you are a doctor; I'm so glad: I want to ask your advice." A bit horrified, I protested my ignorance and tried to explain what Ph.D. implied. No good. She said, "But you must know a lot, and can help me. I am going to be married next week and I want to know what I ought to know—about things." '

'Goodness!' I exclaimed once more. 'What did you answer?'

'I told her just what I would like a girl to know if I were going to marry her.'

I think I deserve a good mark for allowing that conversation to be broken off for ever by a woman who could not make up her mind whether to cross the road or not; after a few tentative steps forth and back she made a wild dash in front of the car, and arrived on the other side, breathless and only just alive.

One does not naturally think of a car-drive as a good setting for conversation, but I found that its very drawbacks may lead to more things being *said*. And another delight I had found in a car: I had been great distances by train and by sea, but never before saw and felt the country round me. In a car you know one county from another by the upkeep of the roads, you sense big distances, you feel every incline. While there are endless things to admire, there is always something to be overcome, and it is conquest of something (if only of low spirits) that keeps one alive.

'You see that long ridge away on the horizon?' said Arthur to me in Wales. 'Well, we've got to get over or round that somehow before candlelight.' Another time, in a wilder part, we found a road with a notice: 'This road is difficult, but not impassable.' 'Let's try it,' said Arthur, and the notice had certainly not been exaggerated.

'Let's try it,' seems to be Arthur's rule of life. By the way, he and Barnholt tried something in the shed one day, and the noise of the explosion was so terrific that even the deaf Mr. K. came running out to know what was the matter, and to give first aid to the survivors.

XII

Sudden Excursions

AMONG our holidays, of which suddenness was a special charm, we count our first visit to Ireland, in 1932.

Our friend Moran, after years of world-wandering, had married and acquired a place in his native land near Lismore. 'Do come over and see how we are coping with the situation,' he wrote, and added, 'There is room for all.'

'All' meant at the moment only Arthur and me. Vivian was tied to his work in London, and Barnholt had gone to South Africa for work on a newspaper. It was fine spring weather, and we didn't hesitate. 'Travel light,' said Arthur, 'for we can't take the car. We must go by Fishguard.'

After a dinner in town we had some time to spare, and went into a cinema. It was my first experience of a 'Talkie' —then in a crude stage of development, for it seemed to me unbearable with its harsh noises.

When we reached Paddington I discovered that in my anxiety to travel light I had actually started without putting on my overcoat. Fortunately Vivian had come to see us off. Always *au fait* in everything to do with railways, he said, 'Oh, that's all right. The Railway Company hire rugs for the journey for a shilling. I'll soon get you one. You just give it up at the other end, or leave it in the carriage.'

No moral consideration would have led me to part from that rug at Fishguard. It was just as well, for our sea-passage was so bad that even the steward was ill. Nor had

I the heart to deliver it up when we reached the Irish port, for I reflected that the railway journey to come might be the better for a rug. There was no need to worry; no one minded what I was carrying. Arthur and I climbed into a carriage of a train that seemed the only one at all likely to start. Its lack of any attempt at comfort reminded me of my childhood's experiences. No, there was one effort to provide comfort—a piece of wood sticking out by the window seat, to form a 'rest' for the elbow. This contrivance was as murderous as Macbeth, and we grinned at one another as each tried to evade it. But my rug, well huddled up, conquered it.

Our pace was leisurely, and stoppages were few, for indeed there seemed to be no towns anywhere. Moran had arranged to meet us at a small station, with his car. When we got out on to an empty platform, I thought, 'If Moran isn't here I shall die.' But he soon appeared, bounding cheerily along, and packed us into his car. Here, too, I was glad of my G.W.R. rug, for I was cold with emptiness.

I believe my worst moment that morning was when Moran put on a record of a jazz dance to welcome us. His wife was more to the point, stirring the log fire and brewing tea.

The approach to the house had been imposing enough, along a curving, wooded drive, up-hill to a spacious frontage, bright with crimson rhododendrons in full bloom. But the house itself could only be described as a mansion. The rooms were lofty, the windows enormous, the staircase grandiose—everything stately. The grounds were in accordance, with old fruit-trees, a brightly flowing stream, devious paths, leading away in a limitless fashion. In a shed we saw a very old donkey, who ought to have been called Petra, for he certainly looked half as old as time. We soon discovered that, in this part of Ireland at least, a donkey is really what Mrs. Elton described as 'a sort of necessity in country life'. Indeed, I feel that if the car had been out of action, the donkey-cart would have been the only alternative.

For the town was a good distance away, and 'deliveries' were scarce. Milk was brought in from a neighbouring farm, but the post came only twice a week, while newspapers, meat, groceries, and all other necessaries of life had to be fetched in the car. So every morning there was a foraging sortie. Arthur and I used to enjoy this, for shopping was not the humdrum affair it is in England. You paid not only money for your goods, but lively conversation as well. One day I suggested making bread at home, and for this yeast was wanted.

'Where shall we get it?' I asked, for all the shops seemed the same to me. There was no baker, or butcher, or grocer, to a stranger's eye. Every shop sold stout and tobacco, and displayed advertisements for emigration, but beyond these there was no guide to their contents or business.

'Oh, we'll get it at Newnam's,' said Moran.

'Ah, now, I have not, but I can soon get it,' was Mr. Newnam's ready assent; 'the boy shall go for it.'

Then followed a bright talk between us all, on the weather, the agricultural outlook, the coming horse races, and so forth. Other customers came in and joined in the discussions, quite unmindful of their errands. At last the boy returned with the yeast.

'How much is it?' I asked; and when after some hesitation the amount was stated, I thanked him, paid it, said good morning, and got into the car.

'You've given great offence in there,' said Moran when at last he came out.

'Whatever have I done?'

'The old chap expected quite half an hour's more talk.'

It was no wonder that Mrs. Moran found cooking a difficult job. By the time Moran had collected the necessaries for dinner there was little left for the cooking of it. And she could not select anything that could be cooked quickly, because 'a lump of meat' (denomination unspecified) was his usual capture.

No shop-keeper was anxious to sell his goods, to arrange them in any order, or to make his window attractive. For instance, one firm in Dublin had closed down just when their goods were in great demand.

'What made you close down?' asked an Englishman.

'Ah,' was the reply in a dissatisfied tone; 'we were getting too many orders.'

We had heard of the beauty of old Waterford glass, and Arthur was anxious to get a specimen of it.

'There are some good bits of it at the inn,' said Moran, 'and the old chap will be glad to sell you some, I'm sure.'

He certainly was glad, and Arthur acquired a beautiful pipette. But a song-cycle would be needed to describe that purchase adequately. Abraham's bargaining with the Hittite for the cave of Machpelah came nowhere near it for courtesy and finesse.

Although the slightest requirements in shopping usually consumed the entire morning, the duty was not allowed to encroach on the afternoons, when we went for drives in the country. Here the great surprise to me was the scarcity of population. A donkey-cart now and again, a basket-laden woman in a black shawl, here and there a few cabins, tumble-down and roofless—these on a long country drive were the main signs of life. 'Look! There's a house!' we would exclaim if we saw one.

It was this very loneliness that (for us at least) added a curious fascination to the scenery of hills and vales, the soft colours, and the delicate cloud effects. Once we pulled up at a bend in a road, high up, where we had a view of almost the whole extent of the county of Tipperary. The words of the song were indeed appropriate, I thought.

Another afternoon we went to Youghall. Moran had seen a notice of a furniture sale there, and hoped to pick up a bargain. While he, Arthur, and Mrs. Moran were in the shop on what I knew would be a long business, I remained parked in the car. The street was deserted, and after I had gazed my full, drowsiness seized me and I fell asleep. Next thing, I was vaguely aware of a kind of hum. There was no voice, but what seemed like the sound of innumerable feet on the ground. Feeling sure that the population of Youghall could hardly produce this effect, and that I had been dreaming, I opened my eyes to find myself completely sur-rounded by humanity—a vast crowd filled the street and was closing up to the car.

'Here am I, actually in the midst of one of these Irish rebellions!' thought I, delightfully excited. But they appeared to have no violent intentions—only a craving to walk, and in silence at that. My bubble of excitement was pricked when Moran came out and told me it was only a 'wake' for some local man.

Another expedition was undertaken merely to satisfy my curiosity. I could not believe that the Trappist Monks could be so absurd as to give up talking for the rest of their days. A silent retreat for a week was possible, but silence for life! I think a woman would rather die out of hand. So Moran and Arthur and I set out.

'They won't let you in to see the monks,' said Moran, 'because you are a woman.'

'Do they make forbidding signs to keep me off?'

'No. One of the monks acts as a porter, and speaks for the rest.'

So when we drew up to the door, this porter-monk passed Moran and Arthur on to visit the whole monastery, and then led me up to a parlour. Here he chatted with me about this and that, and astonished me by asking where I lived, what I did, how I carried on, and what Cuffley was like! Gossip, no less. Meanwhile Moran and Arthur had been shown the monks at their meal, at their bakery, at their work in the fields, at their washing, &c. Not, I fancy, that there is much washing of clothes; for apparently each new disciple is given a garment when he enters, and keeps it until it serves as a shroud. Believe it or not, one of their number was a London stockbroker.

My love of Ireland is very likely based on my Cornish

ancestry—to some deep-lying pre-Celtic affinity. Everything in Ireland seems ancient. Even the trees have a venerable look, some of them almost terrifying, as if they had 'seen things not to be spoken of'. The sight that moved me most profoundly in Ireland was a stone poised on three others, called locally 'the cromlech' (not far from Dublin). It was just like one near our old home in Cornwall. These are believed to be relics of a religion older than that of the Druids. I went up to it and laid my hand on the great top boulder, thinking of the tears of the mothers whose sons had been sacrificed on it, to propitiate God in some way—not so very different from any other religious rite. Something 'numinous' clung still to this old altar, and the fact that a goal-post stood only a few feet away rather enhanced than lessened its dignity.

Moran is one of the world's natural wanderers, and soon left his beautiful house and grounds to come to England. But Arthur did the reverse turn, and is now settled in Ireland. He has told me several stories about the Irish, one of which pleases me so much that I must repeat it: An Irish preacher was inveighing against drink, and in describing its ill effects he said, 'What is it that makes you quarrel with a man? The Drink. What is it that makes you swear at 'm? The Drink. What is it that makes you put up your gun to shoot at 'm? The Drink. And what makes you miss 'm? The Drink.'

Many a holiday that Arthur offered to take me I had refused—even one to Italy (very tantalizing). But one to Cornwall I could not resist. An old Cambridge friend invited both of us to stay with his people in Grampound.

The Riley rubbed its hands at the idea, and off we went. Our kind hosts were quite willing for me to go off where I liked, and one day when the boys were going to the Land's End I asked them to drop me within walking distance of Reskadinnick, my mother's old home. I didn't want to drive up in a car, but to wander along the lanes I had raced about as a child. Nothing had changed at all, and I made my way through the old stable-yard (once made perilous by the turkey-cock), past the dairy, and walked in at the kitchen door. There sat my cousin Lucy, shelling peas.

'Molly!' she cried, as if she had seen a ghost, and flung her arms round me.

'Just ten minutes,' said I, fearing that an extra to dinner might be tiresome.

'Nonsense,' said Lucy, 'there's a couple of fowls on the boil for dinner, and if you give me a hand with these peas, we'll put them on at once.'

'I'm not really in a hurry,' said I; 'the people I'm staying with have Cornish hospitality and don't fuss you. I'll get an afternoon train.'

'That's grand. Frank is in the kitchen garden; he'll be delighted to see you. He's writing the history of something, and has got into difficulties with his typewriter.'

We had a glorious feast of food and talk and laughter. Lucy had transformed the old 'front kitchen' into a dining-room, but keeping its cottage character, and I couldn't possibly have imagined a happier last visit to the beloved old home.

It was not long after this that Lucy and her husband found the place too large for them to manage, and put it on the market for sale. To my deep satisfaction it was bought by a man who had known it as a boy, had been kindly entertained by my Aunt Tony, and had always wished to live in it. So dear old Reskadinnick can still keep smiling.

There is one spot in Cornwall dearer than any other to me, and Arthur (knowing this) proposed one day that we should go alone to Hell's Mouth, to look down into the sea from this dangerous bit of the North Cliffs. As I ran up the bank ahead of Arthur, he called out to me to take care, for to anyone coming up behind it looks as if another step *must* take you over the edge. How strangely his words reminded me of his father's anxiety about me at the same place fifty years before. It had now become a spot for charabancs to unload their tourists, and on the grassy slope we found a shed for the sale of 'minerals' and 'Hell's Mouth Rock', all pink and white!

The Riley is still going strong, consuming much petrol to the mile, and much oil, but rattling heartily through the streets of Dublin, to the amusement of Arthur's friends. The hood-flaps and the windows give more ventilation than necessary, but the Riley engine looks like lasting for ever.

Meanwhile Hilda had not only become a proficient driver; she had bought a car; and we had many an expedition together. One of these was over the Butter-tubs Pass. The hills were showing that lovely combination of snow, grey grass, and mist. While I was gazing round at this, Hilda was gazing round (this side and that) at the road, which was that horrible combination of snow, ice, and slush. When we reached the top a gloomy Yorkshire yokel informed us that 'yon road' was a bad one. And he was right. Going up is child's play to going down a slippery slope. Hilda silently crept on, and we were so near the edge of the terrace road, that I expected we should slip over at any moment. At the bottom we ran into a dense fog. Again Hilda crept on, while I leant out and reported how far we were from the edge.

'There's a car ahead,' cried Hilda. 'What luck! I shall just follow him.'

'But he mayn't be going our way,' I protested.

'Never mind. He must be going somewhere, which is more than we are.'

Petrol-pumps are supposed to be ugly, but what more joyful sight can be imagined when you are out of petrol or have lost your way? We drew up at a garage, just as the fog was lifting.

'Which way for Middlesbrough?' I called out.

'You're in it,' came back with a grin.

What odd bits of pleasure stick in one's memory, when weightier matters are forgotten. The words of that garage man were sweeter to me than the beauties of the Butter-tubs Pass. A visit to Bury St. Edmunds would have faded into the background, if it hadn't been for a satisfying lunch, after a long drive, at the *Angel*, in which the first course was 'a soup with a message' (to use an expression of Barnholt's).

One expedition with Hilda has taken on the tone, in retrospect, of a happy dream. She was anxious to visit the scene of her father's childhood. The very name of the place was fascinating. It was a village called Winfarthing, near Diss, in Norfolk. That was all we knew, as we set forth, equipped with an A.A. map and a picnic lunch. Neither of us being good at reading a map, we were suddenly shaken with doubt while bowling along a good road. At the corner where a lane turned off stood that glorious old sight—a blacksmith's forge.

Glad of an excuse to speak to the man, we pulled up and asked the way to Diss. He seemed equally glad of a chat, and offered much advice. But in the end it boiled down to 'Take this 'ere lane'.

We took it, and how we have tried to pin it down in our memory so that we might find it again. But I think it will always elude us. It was definitely a dream lane. Scotland and Wales and Ireland have their grandeurs, but there is something about a completely countrified English lane that touches the heart more than all of them—the sleepy old cottages, the green hedgerows, the warm glow of haystacks, the comfortable cattle, the blue distances, the feeling of peace in every direction. Perhaps the feeling is akin to our rapture in looking at the face of a child—the certainty that the beauty cannot last for long.

We were sure that the lane had been anything but the shortest way, and were cheered at last to see 'Diss' on a signpost. A funny name, and we wondered whether it was Flemish in origin, for the place had once been famous for its hempen cloth. On we pushed to Winfarthing—an English name if ever there was one. As it stands out in my memory, it consists of only a church and some six or seven houses. While Hilda was paying a formal visit at the rectory, I went into the church and tried to reconstruct the scene when my old friend was a small boy, listening to his father's sermon. Then I went into the short village street, and had a chat with a very old woman leaning over a gate, obviously curious about any people who came in a car. She remembered Mr. Bourne, and even his father, but was too old to be really coherent. In the Post Office I learnt much more about the family in old days, and was able to bring the postmistress up to date about Mr. Bourne and his brothers. Hilda soon joined me, and we bought postcards of the church and village, and posted them off to South Africa. Her grandfather's memory was a sacred one in Winfarthing, for he had continued to visit the sick and dying during an epidemic of small-pox, at the cost of his own life.

We started for home with but one firm resolution—to avoid Chelmsford. Not that we had any animus against it as a town, but we had found it a bunker on our way out. As we drew near its danger zone it was getting dusk, and several times I had to jump out to read the sign-post. 'To Chelmsford', I called out again and again. Hilda went back a bit each time to try another turning. It seemed funny at first, but after a while it took on an unpleasant tone, reminding me of a nightmare story I was told when a child. This pretty tale described a party of travellers riding through unknown country. One rider got left behind for some reason, rode after them, skirting the edge of a forest; after some time he was cheered to see the marks of a horse's hoofs, and galloped on in confidence; after some time again he saw the marks of two horses; still more cheered he galloped on again; but when he counted the marks of three horses, the awful truth dawned on him that he had been riding round the forest, and the hoof-marks were those of his own horse. Not a tale fit for a child, I think, for no happy ending followed.

But Hilda and I did escape Chelmsford, saw 'Epping' on a post, and got home before nightfall.

Hilda had been shown Oxford and Cambridge, Salisbury and Winchester, scenery of Wales and Yorkshire, and much more. But she declared one day that she must see the city of York properly, to which (she understood) no other town could hold a candle. It was June, so I calculated that if we started early we could reach York in time for a good look round before dark, spend the night at an hotel, and have the next morning for another stare before coming home.

So off we set, with a bite of lunch in the car, and went ahead like Young Lochinvar, staying not for scenery and stopping not for tea. Fearing that Hilda might be tired, I offered her some other towns, attractive enough, through which we passed. She gave me such an ugly look at each suggestion, that I told her the story of the captain taking his ship from Dublin to Wales on an appalling night. The storm was too bad for him to stop to drop the pilot, and he met all protest with the words, 'It's Holyhead or Hell for you to-night, my man.'

'Yes,' laughed Hilda, 'it's York or Hell for you to-night, Voom.'

It would be thought impossible to go wrong on the historic road to York, but Hilda had a passion for short cuts, and once we found ourselves against an extraordinary obstacle: a bridge was being repaired, and a notice said,

'Speed not to exceed two miles an hour.' Difficult to walk at this rate, but to make a car go impossible. Not even Lochinvar would have ventured past a man with a red flag, so we stopped and laughed. But the flag-man was more kindly than he looked, and soon allowed us to stagger past at about ten miles per hour.

We ran into York in full daylight, and looked about for an hotel. A nice little quiet one was our idea. The A.A. book had not been of much use, for each hotel quoted seemed too starry for our purse. The traffic was congested in the narrow streets, and our progress was slow, but no hotel could we see that struck the right note. At last I got an idea.

'You see that genial-looking policeman over there, Hilly? Pull up and I'll get across and ask his advice.'

He was all smiles and acquiescence when I told him our trouble. 'I know the very thing for you, and you can reach it without turning the car. You will have comfortable beds and good meals, and if you say that Nelson sent you, there will be a hearty welcome.'

'What finer name than yours for a passport!' said I.

The welcome and everything was just as he predicted, and believe me the name of the little road in which this inn lay was Whip-ma-Whop-ma-Gate. After a hearty York-shire tea we wandered out again into the town, among its alleys and by-ways, leaving the Minster for the morning. On returning we were faced with an enormous dinner. I found that Hilda preferred wandering about the city to studying the Minster, so our next morning consisted chiefly in resisting the attractions of old curiosity shops—brasses and china that would gladden anyone. It was a Yorkshire cottager who was found by my sister-in-law bemoaning that she was short of cups and saucers, and company coming to tea and all. 'But why not use those cups on your dresser?' was the natural remark. 'No, no, I want my dresser to be viewly.' Such a lovely word must not be lost, and I mutter it to myself sometimes as I look at my old Welsh dresser and its contents.

One day in Cambridge Arthur heard two of his friends, just before the Easter vac., lamenting that they couldn't afford to go to Hungary to see their mother. Arthur broke in:

'It would reduce travelling expenses a lot if I drove you home in my Riley. It's easy enough to ship a car over to the Continent if you just leave it entirely to the A.A. They look after it and you and all as if you were a baby in arms.'

To their polite protests Arthur replied that he wanted to have a look at some foreign universities and labs, and without their introductions he would be helpless. 'I can speak a bit of German, if you give me time,' he added, 'but I can't argue with a garage man, or explain what the Riley wants—you'll have to do all that.'

Arthur had been elected to a Beit Fellowship, which required him to carry on research work either at Cambridge or anywhere in the world he liked, so this trip with fellow students would be all to the good. I was delighted at the suggestion, for the two men had come to see us at Cuffley, and I had found them all that one could desire.

Without their aid the trip through middle Europe would have been more hazardous than it actually was. It was true that 'peace had broken out in the Balkans', but there were symptoms of local warfare here and there. This was in 1934, and they noticed German troops ominously near the Austro-German frontier, and everything seemed to be creaking badly. Coming late at night into one town they found the road barred by wire stretched across it. Arthur had been driving very cautiously or there would have been a bad accident.

The farther he went the more fascinating the places and people appeared to be. 'I was terribly sorry to leave Nuremburg,' he wrote to me, 'then into Austria to Linz and Wien (spell it with a Wee, Sammy). From Linz to Wien we drove the last hundred miles along the Danube in full moonlight; and it was worth coming a thousand miles, even if only to sneer at people who chat about the Rhine.' (This remark reminded me of Barnholt's Kilimanjaro.) 'According to Farkas,' Arthur continued, 'everything still to come is better than wherever we happen to be, and he has been right so far.' Arthur's idea of the Austrians was that they were infinitely more charming than the Germans, and full of fun, giving the impression, like ourselves, of not caring really much what happens.

At last came a letter from Budapest, and he wrote: 'An extraordinary place this; it's the last bit of Western civilization as you go East, and the people are just charming. It's a great difference being here with two natives—one doesn't feel such a rubberneck, and general existence is much easier when it comes to mundane details such as eating and drinking and greasing the car. The people look absolutely different from others, and their manners are far superior to any others in Europe. They are certainly the most generally prosperous people I've met yet, largely because they're almost entirely agricultural folk, with no huge industrialized class. Their chief groan is, of course, that more than half of Hungary is no longer Hungary, but Rumanian or Italian or Czech. Their port on the Danube, Bratislava, is now in Czechoslovakia; their old capital (corresponding to Winchester) is now bang in the middle of Rumania, and so on; and of course they have lost their sea at Trieste. These are the people I would least like exterminated in Europe.'

On the way back several universities were visited, and useful information sucked from them. But Arthur was not satisfied with his life of research; it was interesting, but might well lead nowhere. So he renounced the Fellowship and applied for a 'job of real work', as he described it, 'where you clock in, and do your bit of useful stuff'. He soon found such a job in Dublin, with definite hours of work, and definite holidays. One of these consisted of three weeks, and he consulted me as to how it should be spent. We thought of all sorts of places, but finally decided on New York—something quite new, unlike anything he had seen before—and, as usual with Arthur, he had several friends over there that he could look up. He sailed in the *Queen Mary* on one of her worst voyages.

'Would you mind sitting perfectly still,' he wrote to me, 'just for two minutes, that I may be sure something will be quite still again.'

America was certainly a new experience, with its slick, fervid haste and its terrifying efficiency. His kindly host in Washington was showing him everything, and about to start for something fresh when Arthur said, 'I'm afraid I mustn't do any more or I shall miss my train to New York, and my boat for England.'

'Your train! What nonsense! I'll phone for a taxi to be here in time to take you to the aerodrome, for a plane in time for your boat. That gives us an hour to spare. Come along.'

So Arthur was the first of the family to fly, and he told me that it was so smooth going that he didn't realize that he was moving at all.

XIII

Living Alone

'BALLOONING.' Such was the title of a short article in a daily paper, in which a middle-aged woman described the delights of being over fifty. She said how continually she was able to throw overboard her old prejudices, her old fears, not to speak of large chunks of her old conscience. And each time something went overboard she felt to be rising into a brighter clime. It struck me as a good idea, and in complete harmony with the advice given us in Holy Writ.

Now, in the middle nineteen-thirties, my cares seemed very few. True, I had still to work for my living, but that I enjoyed. The boys were all independent, and consequently at last 'out of hand', as the Victorians used to say when a child could walk steadily, avoid fire and matches, and navigate the stairs.

Not but what the boys had plenty of troubles of their own, but that is their story, exciting enough indeed, but outside my canvas. They wrote frequently, and dropped in at any odd chance of a holiday. Once even, in '37, Barnholt snatched a breather from South Africa.

Otherwise I live entirely alone—more so than if I lived in one of the neighbouring houses, for no one passing along the road would imagine that there was a house here. In this way I am spared many visits from hawkers and sellers of stationery or vacuum cleaners. My old friend Harris continues to come with his pony-cart, and I rack my brains to think of something to buy from him. And I found another friend in 'the vinegar man' (as he is generally known), whom I call my wine merchant, for he sells home-made sloe wine, which the boys declare to be guaranteed free from alcohol. One day this Mr. de Liége brought his daughter, a charming little girl. I invited her in, for I know how dearly a child loves to see what other people's houses are like. She reported at home that I had 'millions of books'. Of course I found her one or two to add to her own collection. She came to see me several times, and so did her mother, and though Mr. de Liége has been translated to a higher sphere in the commercial world, they all come to see me when they can.

One periodical caller was a complete contrast. He sold household goods—sheets, curtains, mats, &c. In an evil hour I gave him an order. After that he pursued his advantage, called often, order-book to the fore, and then talked incessantly. Even if I ordered something to get rid of him he felt it only courteous to keep on talking. Once I told him that I was stirring the marmalade and feared it would burn. No good: he came and stirred the marmalade for me. Fortunately he called one day when the gardener was here, and I think must have had the truth told him, for he has not been since.

This gardener, Mr. Sale, has been my stand-by, adviser, and helper for some fifteen years. Once a week he has done the garden, while his wife did the house. He looks upon the garden as his own creation, arranging flowers and plants for me to come upon in surprise, putting in any trees I fancy, pruning the fruit-trees so that I get a good store of apples, mending anything that goes wrong in the house, whitewashing the kitchen, planting vegetables that he does not charge for, because he has 'acquired' them. He seems to act as a liaison officer between the gardens he tends. On the few occasions when I have been ill, he and his wife were at once by my side. He has provided me with various nooks (to suit all winds and weathers), where I can do examination papers in peace. I remember one morning finding Thermo, the kitten, fast asleep in one of the big university envelopes. Among other things, Mr. Sale converted a natural pond into a respectable, rockery-edged, lily-decked affair. For this Arthur bought half a dozen sixpenny goldfish. Before long these had multiplied into a countless multitude; but by some compensating power of nature, into which it is unpleasant to inquire, they were soon reduced to about fifty. For years these became charming companions, so tame that they would feed out of my hand, swimming eagerly up as soon as I came near the pond. Altogether a grand resource for amusing children or for providing conversation with a heavy-going visitor. It was a real grief to me when quite recently they all disappeared except four—and these four so shy that they hid under weeds or rocks if anyone approached. None of the old camaraderie. Each of my friends had a separate theory about this slaughter. But the conclusion most favoured was Mr. K.'s. He had seen a kingfisher hovering over his own pond, and described with horrid realism the methods of this bird. But I would have been glad to sacrifice a few fish if I could have seen a kingfisher—a sight hitherto denied me.

At one of the schools I was inspecting the teachers told me that they made excursions to Cuffley for studying bird-life. I was not surprised, for I had counted a large variety in the garden alone—robin, wren, thrush, blackbird, tree-pipit, wood-pigeon, starling, finch, wagtail, tomtit, martin, magpie, plover, rook, *and* sparrow. As for the lark over our adjoining field, and the nightingale in the near-by trees, their songs have kept me rejoicing as I have lain awake morning and night during their season—the nightingale being far rarer than the lark.

There is no shyness about most of these birds. Finches and tits tap on the window for food, while robins hop right into the room for crumbs, and this year a blackbird came in and proceeded to feed its offspring—rather larger than itself. Hens from the adjoining farm are not so welcome. They eat up my young greenstuff, scratch over the beds, and have no idea that you are tired of them, even when you throw a stone at them. And never an egg is laid.

Alien animals have been frequent. Horses have got in and trampled down newly-laid lawn and beds. Cows and sheep have pushed through the hedge to sample our grass. Pigs have galumphed about, for the sheer love of aggression. Stray cats and dogs are so frequent as to be nothing accounted of; they like to examine our bresh-heap. One morning I was excited to see round the house the marks of a fox's pad in the snow; and another time the pack of hounds were running through the garden. Several times I have seen a cock pheasant, a magnificent fellow, stepping delicately round the garden, like some Eastern potentate looking for a good site for a palace.

Each tree and shrub in the garden is a personal friend, for
it is either a venerable oak, gorse, may-tree, or crab-apple,
or else it is one we have brought from the wood or 'acquired'
through Mr. Sale; these new-comers are birches, beeches,
rowans, willows, poplars, rhododendrons, wisteria, honey-
suckle, jasmine, syringa, berberis, and holly. But the ones
I love best are the Scotch firs, that I planted a foot high;
they now form a dignified little plantation of large spreading
branches, pink barks, and generous cones.

As the house is in rather an exposed spot, and very high,
we get great variety of weather—crashing thunderstorms,
superb rainbows, tearing winds, fine summer heat, and great
snow-drifts. At the moment our pipes are frozen, and we
are anxiously awaiting the plumber. Vivian is with me for
a few days, and has hacked out a path through the deep
snow in the drive. For days he had to fetch water from
Mrs. K. in buckets. I never can see the beauty of snow.
Its by-products are so unpleasant. When people get
ecstatic about it I remember the story of the man who
remained unmoved by a capital joke while all around were
laughing. 'Good story, that?' said one of them to him, and
his reply was, 'I can see no fun in a man who owes me five
pounds.'

Except for weather that brings slush and broken pipes,
I enjoy every turn of the seasons. Our sky effects are end-
lessly attractive from dawn to dusk, especially the unexpected pink light in the East that often appears after sunset.
And at night we get old Orion, or the sickle of the waning
moon, and the cheerful glow of light from the streets of
London.

Strange as it may seem, November is one of my favourite months. People who abuse it are town-dwellers, who have settled down to winter gloom, and get their best fun in preparing for Christmas. When returning from London in November I am always struck by the contrast between the grimy, leafless trees of the town and the golden colour of the oaks as I come near Cuffley; and a walk in the woods is a feast of colour-effects from the oaks, the beeches, the bracken, and the elegant white barks of the birches. And the birds seem to agree with me; or else why do they sing so gaily in November? I should like to have a scientific opinion on this. We are always being told that birds don't sing for joy, but for some sordid economic end. Now in November surely their family cares are over? And their song can have no blooming merit about it? Surely it is possible for them to feel just jolly, as we humans do, for no earthly reason.

And there's always this to be said for November—next month the days will begin to lengthen.

Cuffley attracts hundreds of hikers and picnickers on every bank holiday. Scouts and guides run about the woods doing what they do do. A coco-nut shy is put up outside the *Plough*. Streams of cars come to see our one special attraction—the monument to Robinson. The Zeppelin had come down so near our house that we had found a bit of its outer casing when we were digging in the garden. And yet, with all this going on, these holidays are the quietest in the year for me. We are too far from the road to hear anything, or for hikers to come to the door for water. No tradesman calls, no visitor ventures, no newspaper troubles the conscience. I sometimes take an odd kind of amusement in walking to the gate in the evening, to watch the crowds making slowly towards the station, sated with the strenuous pleasures of Cuffley.

When I am driven indoors through stress of weather, time never hangs heavy. A batch of examination papers and a pile of books waiting for review provide work, and sometimes fun. (A girl once in quoting Shakespeare by request wrote of the toad as 'ugly and verminous'.) Interspersed with household jobs, no brainwork can become irksome. And a telephone call has still a pleasurable excitement: it has often meant one of my old schoolfellows adumbrating a visit to me—Bessie Jones from Enfield, Mary Wood or her sister Ursula from London, or one of my newly-acquired friends from inspections, or an old pupil such as Violet Gask (whose respect had waned but affection endured). A strange voice on the phone one day was peremptory: 'Mrs. Bloggs speaking. Kindly send me up a pint of milk.'

'Sorry,' said I, 'but I cannot spare it; I've only just enough for myself.'

'What! And you call yourself a dairy!'

'No, I don't. You never asked me who I was.'

The drawback to phone calls is that you put down your pen somewhere on the way, and can't find it afterwards.

One constant though rare visitor is my sister-in-law, Carrie. Two or three times a year she drives in her car from Middlesbrough and breezes in to take care of me and the house generally. She treats me to surprise cookings, helps me to do *The Times* crossword over lunch, takes me for a drive in the afternoons, and does a bit of mending for me in the evenings. Epping Forest is our favourite place for our picnic tea, pitched near the spot where I was born. Once I was so pressed for time that I had to take a batch of examination papers to the forest.

A continual solace indoors is the wireless. After sturdy refusal on my part for years, the boys insisted on giving me a set. I have sometimes, when alone, found myself dancing about the room to a really good dance-tune. But the greatest pleasure of all has come from the concerts at Queen's Hall. Brahms' Second Symphony, or Beethoven's Fifth, is my greatest favourite, or the Eighth—each in its way the best. But Carrie loves the Seventh, and the Presto movement, which she calls, 'Go to blazes and visit your aunt.'

Of course the best time of all is when one of the boys blows in. They insist on some improvement—the installation of electric light, or a thing for giving constant hot water, and Arthur is always agitating for a refrigerator. They take me to a theatre or a film. The rareness of this last treat can be judged by a remark of mine during some show:

'That's a good-looking girl,' I whispered, 'that one just come in.'

'Good-looking girl!' gasped Arthur. 'Why, that's Greta Garbo.'

One entertainment I am sure of if any one of the boys appears—a game of chess. We play 'gloves off', with no nonsense of a warning of the queen in danger, or having a move back. I usually lose, but if I win, the next game starts with the threat to me, 'Now I'm going to wipe the floor with you, Voom.'

This nickname came to me from the income-tax collector, who for years has insisted on addressing his unwelcome communications to Mrs. V. M. Hughes. I exclaimed in annoyance one day, 'V. M. indeed! It sounds like Mrs. Voom Hughes.'

'It's the very name for you,' said Arthur, 'it sounds like a fast car passing one in the road.' And so the name stuck.

One day an odd chance made a great difference to me. Among the books sent to me for review was one which I had long shirked. Anxious to get it out of the way, at last I seized it, and wrote a few words along the well-worn lines: 'This book will be read with pleasure by those who enjoy this type of reminiscence.' An introductory note by some well-known person spoke of it as 'gracious', 'tender', and 'delicate', or some such words. By the way, I always suspect a book that needs someone else to induce you to read it. The book described the early days of some children, generally good, and sometimes prettily naughty. 'Good heavens,' I thought, 'there was nothing delicate or tender about my own childhood, but it was certainly full-blooded enough to be as entertaining as this book.' From that moment I began to recall the jolly days of our old home and the doings of my brothers, and the oddities of our parents.

After some weeks I had a pile of jottings on scraps of paper, and these I sorted into separate envelopes, according to a plan that Barnholt had taught me for preparing any book. When I had material for some dozen chapters, I got out the type-writer, and began. I was alone for some time and got ahead with it. I did not care to expose it to the view of my sons, for I feel sure that they are always secretly nervous that their mother is being silly. Their motto seems to be: 'It is better to remain silent and be thought a fool, than to open your mouth and remove all doubt.'

But when Carrie next came I submitted a chapter to her. She is always far too encouraging, but even she saw no hope of my getting the thing published, since I had known no famous people, nor had any terrific adventures. But she urged me to type it all out, for the boys to keep against the day when they might possibly be interested in it.

It was great fun writing it, anyhow; but as it was quite out of the question to get it published, I pitched on the publisher in London of the oldest standing, and whom I considered the most world-famous, in the spirit of 'as well be hanged for a sheep as a lamb'. Did he think, I wrote, that a book about a Victorian childhood would be suitable for his list? Definitely *not* was his reply, but he added that he would look at it if I chose to submit it.

'How nice and polite of him,' thought I, and packed it off. It was like those tyres that you fit and forget. I gave the thing not a second thought, and when after several weeks I received a letter proposing to publish the book, it is hardly an exaggeration to say that I nearly fell down with amazement.

Another surprise came later. In the case of my former books, my wealth consisted mainly in the pleasure of getting the material. But in this story of my childhood my wealth consisted mainly in the number of new friends it brought me. No, not admirers of my literary style (of which Barnholt declared me to be entirely innocent), but people who had

had similar fun and similar troubles as children, or recognized places and persons that I had had no need to disguise. In short, the book revived their *own* memories, delightful in retrospect, and they were kind enough to write and thank me. Some of these friends were visible (for they actually came to Cuffley to see me); others were invisible.

Among the visible ones was a doctor, who undertook a double railway journey, to bring me fine photographs he had taken of my own old home and adjoining places I had mentioned. He had been born a few doors away from our house, and was four days older than myself. He had photographs, too, of some old broad-gauge G.W.R. trains, like those in which he and I had travelled to Cornwall ages long ago.

Another visible friend was a Magistrate of Toronto, in England on a visit. He brought his wife to see us; several of us were at home, and we had tea on the lawn. He took a cinematograph of us passing round cakes and pouring out tea. He had liked the book because of an aunt I described who was like a beloved one in his own family. He had actually made a pilgrimage to her old home in Cornwall, in order to tell me how it was looking. How good of him! But no aunt (nor woman, for that matter) was ever equal in goodness to my aunt.

The visibility of another new friend happened at the Army and Navy Stores, where we met for tea. He and his son entertained Hilda and me, not only to tea but afterwards to the Passion Music in St. Paul's. I told him how desirous I had always been to hear this, ever since my brothers had described the shout of 'Barabbas'. (Of course I had never been allowed to go to it as a child.) Then he told me how he had actually joined in the shout, as he had been a choir-boy. But during our talk at tea the main fun came from our gossipy recollections of the services in the Cathedral when we were children. This staid clergyman had much juicier stories to tell me than I had put in the book.

In quite another connexion I was invited by a well-known author to lunch with her at the Pioneer Club, to meet some distinguished people. She had discovered that we were Cornish cousins, and had no end of things in common—not, be it noted, in the literary world, but as Cornishwomen.

The most remote of all my new friends lives in Brisbane; but she came out to Cuffley to see me on her visit to England, and I showed her our wood—a delight she still refers to in her letters.

One who is semi-visible, as it were, is an old acquaintance of the family living in Wales. I must have seen her once at least, for she wrote to say how my book recalled a visit to our house when she was a little girl, and she had always remembered what a kind boy my brother Tom had proved to be in her shyness.

It was my brother Tom, too, who interested one of my invisible friends. She and her mother live in Brooklyn, and although unseen are counted among my best friends.

A coeval of mine in British Columbia told me that she was reading my book one day when she let out such a scream that the family ran up in alarm. It was only a cry of joy because I had been made to learn by heart a long poem from which she herself had suffered. Another friend wrote to say that she had learnt geography out of the same absurd book that I had; and another that she had treasured the same little book of illuminated Scripture texts.

A very welcome letter told me that my mother's odd remarks reminded the writer of the remarks her *own* mother used to make, and she regaled me with several of these. Another reader, older than myself, told me that she was looking forward to meeting my mother in heaven.

A man who had lived in the adjoining road to ours wrote to say that many a time he had passed the high wall of our garden, and thrown back one of our cricket-balls that had come over. This, for some reason, touched my heart very closely. My talk of cricket, too, had brought me a letter from a leading cricketer of the old days, who had crossed the ocean with our childhood's friend, Charlie Absalom, *en route* to fight the Australians. And to my great delight it turned out that our neighbour, the Colonel, had played cricket with Charlie Absalom in the Bermudas; and he wrote me a letter to describe the match.

A teacher whom I had inspected wrote to say that she had read bits aloud to her class, and was greeted with shouts of laughter. I make no doubt that these little scoundrels were gleeful to hear that their awesome inspector had had immense trouble over her arithmetic and sewing, and had been of the opinion that the Romans could well have managed without the Passive Voice.

It is easily seen that in all cases the pleasure derived from the book was due to something in the life of the reader that corroborated what I had said. How glad I was that I had described only real things and real people, real feelings and real places.

I must mention one letter that assumed the proportions of a testimonial. A mother described how all her family had enjoyed the book, adding that she herself was going to enjoy life and its difficulties as never before—much of it due to me. Then followed the signatures of each—herself and her four daughters and her little boy of seven. This last was a rather shakily written 'Nicolas'.

I felt like Humpty Dumpty—'there's glory for you'.

XIV

New-comers

THERE was much to be said for Laocoön's warning. The wooden horse no doubt in the long run led to the introduction of Greek civilization into Troy; but it must have been a painful process for the Trojans at the time. During the twenty years that we have lived in Cuffley, civilization has been creeping into it. We say aloud, and try to feel, how good it is that town-dwellers should come out to live in this healthy spot. But we can't help noticing our own loss in the process.

For years after our settling here a great feature of our pleasure was the unusual beauty of our walks. There were two specially shown to visitors with pride: our star turn was a long grassy glade through the woods, with its varying colours; especially when the season was right for striking a secret route across a field into a copse thick with wild hyacinth. A walk in another direction was almost as good, for it was across fields and over stiles, up and down hill, past a real farm, and producing in spring at one stage in the walk a generous show of daffodils.

And in the autumn we could roam the fields close at hand for mushrooms—more than we could consume; while for blackberries we hardly needed to do more than push out our hand.

But now we are met with barbed wire, notices to keep

to the pathway, to beware of the dogs, 'You have been warned', and other such chilling deterrents.

New houses were springing up so rapidly that after a few days' absence I would find a street of villas along a road that I had regarded as a country lane. Mrs. K. assured me that one would see scaffolding up one day, and curtains in the windows on the next; but this was her heated imagination. It was not the decent villas that troubled us so much as the rows of bungalows built rather tiresomely on the same design. But each one is perhaps a happy home, and the gardens that surround them are marvels of colour; and the little children to be seen about are marvels of health.

Of course we owe to the influx of new people several modern conveniences; more trains have been put on, and one, known as the 'Cuffley Flier', actually runs through Finsbury Park without stopping. The station, instead of lurking in a shapeless bit of lane, now has a station approach, and the station staff is too dignified to make jokes. When I have things sent from a shop in London, 'Cuffley' is understood, and I have now no need to add 'where the Zeppelins go to'.

A row of shops has sprung up, as well as an imposing telephone exchange building, a grand hotel, as well as two or three cafés, and a red car has taken the place of the postman's bicycle. Moreover, sites have been bought for a bank and a Free Evangelical church; we hope that it will be some time yet before they materialize. A few street lamps have been put up, gravel paths are provided along the built-up areas, and a speed-limit board or two erected (to which, by the way, no motorist pays the slightest attention). Now and again we have the steam-roller, and our road has risen to the dignity of B 157. This last is no empty honour, for it has always been difficult to direct a visitor coming to see us by car. It is only recently indeed that the word Cuffley appeared on any sign-post. But, although the name has been put up here and there, the route is still tricky, for our chief road takes many sudden turns that shake the confidence of a driver. Now we have only to say: Take A 1 till you reach B 157, and glue yourself to that (refusing all substitutes) till you come to East Ridgeway, and Fronwen is the first gate you see. A man driver will arrive on time, but we cannot trust a woman driver not to be inveigled by 'To Cuffley' on sundry posts, leading her along very twisty ways, third-rate surfaces, and finally our nasty hill; she is apt to arrive late and a little disordered, not to say a little aggrieved, protesting, 'It *said* "To Cuffley" at Potter's Bar.'

Fortunately that hill of ours is too steep to tempt a bus route, but cars are so plentiful that it is almost a distinction to be without one. When I suggested to Mr. Harris one day that he might be glad of a car to carry his goods he replied, 'I like my pony-cart better—know where you are.' Then he added in an undertone, 'There's lots of these 'ere cars that ain't paid for.'

Social distinction is very much alive in Cuffley, although it no longer depends on the possession of a car. Recently an elementary school has been built near the railway line, well away from dwelling-houses. But the inhabitants of a street of bungalows nearest to it showed a proper spirit by protesting that they could no longer endure such an outrage to their respectability—they must sell their houses, &c. But so far they have not pursued the matter. Is it possible that they find the voices of jolly little children on the way to school quite supportable, if not an asset?

In earlier days at Cuffley the main social affair for all was a meeting of the Conservative Association in the iron schoolroom. The member would appear, breathless from some 'important work in the House', to say a few stirring words, punctuated by thumps from umbrellas when the Prime Minister was mentioned. We used to cull much fun from these. But a still livelier function nowadays is a meeting of our Rate-payers' Association, where real feelings run high, and real words are used.

And then, naturally, a Women's Institute has sprung up, making gallant efforts at culture and craft, with visiting lecturers, competitions, and teas. I hear that there is also a League of Health and Beauty. When I add that there is a district nurse, that one man at least has a television set, and that a telephone booth has been installed near the *Plough*, I think I have exhausted the amenities of Cuffley up to date.

'He loved and he rode away' has a certain poignancy, but after all a girl can still hope. When a speculative builder builds and goes away it is far more poignant. I do not refer to the obvious troubles of poor foundations, ramshackle walls, and general preparations for future slums. These troubles cry to heaven in too many districts to need describing. Cuffley has a peculiar grievance of its own. An attractive new 'estate' appeared, was inhabited at once, and was soon enriched with delightful little gardens. One great advantage had been that the houses, although at the top of the hill, were 'two minutes from the station'. Believe me, this was actually true, if you ran hard. But it depended on a narrow path that gave a short cut. This little cut passed (for a few yards) an older house. The owner of this older house bought the bit of land that the few train-goers had to navigate. He then barricaded the way with strong interlacings of barbed wire. The residents had no remedy against the builder who had gaily promised them this short cut; he had gone away, to build houses and promise amenities in another neighbourhood. But what is barbed wire to men who have been through the War? They soon had it down. It may be supposed that the barbed-wire operator immediately appealed to the law for damages. But he did nothing except make the path so narrow that one has to walk almost sideways to get along. No doubt he has the ordinary man's dread of going to law, lest a worse thing happen to him. At present the situation is delicate and amusing—except for the early morning men who may suddenly find themselves obstructed one day, and be obliged to go round the far longer way.

All Cuffley's activities of a social and elevating kind were frozen stiff that morning in September '39, when the voice of Mr. Chamberlain on the wireless announced sadly: 'We are at war with Germany.' No one has the least idea what the outcome will be, and I am inclined to wonder whether this little community, created by a German air fighter, will be destroyed by another. Meanwhile, we can enjoy its present life while it lasts. Still there is the fresh, bracing air, still there is the green belt between us and the town, still there are all the birds.

Still, too, I am not ashamed to add, there is a little local gossip to be enjoyed. My chief aider and abetter in this indulgence is Mrs. K. We neither of us ever go into our neighbours' houses, and yet we know a good deal about them. The boys call Mrs. K.'s house the Vatican, for she never seems to leave it, and yet knows all that goes on. We attribute this intimate knowledge to the fact that her husband is frequently called in to undertake the healing of leaking roofs, subsidence of foundations, ill-fitting doors and windows, and similar troubles left by the builders who built and went away. He has a great advantage over normal people in being slightly deaf. I fancy that deaf people hear what is spoken loudly to them, and also what is frequently added in a lower tone and not intended for them. Also their eyes are much sharper than those of normal people. Promptitude or the reverse in paying bills is another eye-opener. No names are mentioned, but we manage to get much fun of a harmless kind. One day Mr. K. came home in great glee. He had been walking along the Ridgeway when a woman owner of a large house, in which he had carried out considerable repairs, thrust a half-crown into his hand with a murmured, 'On account.' This half-crown he treasures as a monument of what Cuffley's ideas of business can descend to.

While Mrs. K. knows everybody's name (and, I suspect, income) I can remember faces, but no names. So I take refuge in smiling, and as Brer Rabbit would say 'sponding howdy' to anyone I recognize. One exceedingly old man everybody knew. He lived in a post-War freak cottage built of wood, near the railway. Meeting him one January 1st

I wished him a happy new year. 'A happy new year to you, my darling,' was his surprising reply. When he reached the age of a hundred, Cuffley fêted him. But almost immediately afterwards a spark from an engine set his cottage on fire, and it was reduced completely to ashes. The old man was uninjured, and readily given hospitality among neighbours. A reporter from one of our brighter daily papers was soon on the scene, to take his photograph. This appeared in the paper next morning, to the delight of all concerned. What puzzled them, however, was a photograph of the cottage, entirely unlike anything ever seen in Cuffley. I knew enough behind the scenes of a newspaper, from what Barnholt had told me, to solve the mystery. Of course the reporter could not take a photograph of a cottage that had been burnt quite to the ground, so the photograph of another little cottage had been inserted instead. No matter, this bit of publicity did good, for the old man was given a room in a comfortable almshouse, where he can smoke and reminisce with cheery companions. The story goes that he is fully convinced that he has passed away, and is now in heaven. What his past life has been I have never inquired, but he seems to have attained the ideal of at least one man who said, 'I want to live so that no one but the undertaker shall be glad of my death.'

Friends of all kinds, new as well as old, are all I care about. A ring on the telephone may always mean a word with one. As I walk along the passage to the little lobby to answer it, I speculate on the possibilities: One of the boys ill? Someone coming to tea? Perhaps the words, 'Are you Cuffley 2026? Hold the line for Dublin.' That means

Arthur's voice will be coming through. Perhaps only a wrong number.

I said that there had been three memorable calls for me, the first being from Cambridge. Here are the other two, both about friends, an old and a new—the newest of all.

My oldest friend of all, Mary Wood, had recently retired from the Principalship of the Training College, and had hardly begun to enjoy her freedom when she was taken ill. Ursula rang up to tell me of her death. I had written her a note, which lay among a pile of letters just in from the evening post. 'I'm too tired to read them all,' she said, 'just give me Molly's.' So she read my little note, and fell asleep, never to wake. I cannot be grateful enough to Ursula for telling me this—a small thing no doubt, but it meant a lot to me. It makes me think of a rule of life with my mother: 'Always pass on little pleasant things to other people, and keep the little unpleasant ones to yourself.'

And now for my newest friend. Telephone rings. 'A telegram for you. Will you take it down? The message is: "Granddaughter all well".'

Now that Mary Caroline can laugh and walk, some friends say that she is like Hilda, and others that she is the image of Arthur.

Since her arrival has come the news from South Africa that Barnholt is married. I am sure to like his wife, for she fixed on April 1st as their wedding-day in order that Barnholt might remember it. And her first letter to me began, 'Dear mother of Barnholt.'

It will be gathered from these reminiscences that we are a wealthy family.